THE CUSTOMER
COMMUNICATION FORMULA

Kind words from clients

"Charlotte was my customer service coach when I first joined a contact center in a medical information role. She observed as I managed customer calls and then coached me on how to improve my customer service skills. I developed a keen interest in learning more about her Customer Communication Formula and her coaching style. Later we worked closely together on a Call Management program for the team.

"I have since moved on from that role. Even so, I find myself still referring to what I learned from Charlotte while I'm:

- Coaching agents and managers
- Communicating with family members
- Communicating in meetings
- Preparing presentations
- Presenting myself professionally on the phone and in person

"I am so glad to know that Charlotte is sharing her formula in the book, *The Customer Communication Formula*. I know you will enjoy learning about the formula and how it can help you in your customer service role, in your career, and your personal life."

SUSAN ALLEN
Compliance professional
(former Customer Service Professional)
North Carolina

"A few years ago, I told Charlotte, 'You owe the world a book.' This is it! I was one of the Customer Service Professionals who used her formula to create positive experiences for customers and by doing so, I advanced in my career as well. I encourage you to use *The Customer Communication Formula* to enhance your customer service and advance your career."

MI KYUNG CHUNG, RN
(former Customer Service Professional)
North Carolina

"Charlotte's formula is powerful! Her coaching equipped me with skills far beyond 'excellent customer service'—to a new level where I meet the customer's unspoken and often emotional needs, as well as their informational needs. Helping others so profoundly, and feeling the positive impact to my customers, creates increased passion for delivering amazing service. Charlotte teaches how to deliver customer service that changes lives. And having these skills has changed my life in countless positive ways—both professionally and personally."

KATIE COLE
Program manager
(former Customer Service Professional)
Florida

"Great customer service has been, is, and always will be a part of the recipe for winning in business. If you are trying to unlock the recipe for best-in-class customer service, Charlotte's new book, *The Customer Communication Formula*, is a must read. The book reveals simple, time-tested, actionable industry best practices to put in place to win with your customers.

"I'm so excited that Charlotte is sharing her wonderful knowledge and expertise on the classic topic of Customer Service. She is an extraordinary coach and friend that I was blessed to have met 10 years ago, when I was a leader in a pharmaceutical company. Something she taught me that I'll never forget is in order to achieve best-in-class customer service and to succeed at life in general: 'Communication is #1.'

"I remember telling Charlotte that she 'should write a book.' I encourage leaders to read this book and connect with Charlotte personally. Invite her to speak to your teams so they can learn firsthand from an authentic and enthusiastic subject matter expert—someone who lives to help others succeed."

PAULA HATTLEY
Former director, pharmaceutical industry
North Carolina

"Charlotte has a way of distilling the essence of human interactions to their core and relaying practical steps to take one's Customer Experience skills from good to exceptional. I'm always looking for new ways to provide exceptional service to our customers. *The Customer Communication Formula* is at the top of my list of tools we will use to take our Customer Experience to the highest level."

PAUL IRVING, MBA
Contact center operations manager
(former Customer Service Professional)
North Carolina

"I met Charlotte through the Google Black Founders Exchange. Her people-centered way and customer driven ideas made me know I had to work with her more! Through my work with Charlotte, I not only saw more clearly through the eyes of my customer, I tapped into my own authentic voice that helped me shape the experience for my team members and customers alike. She gave me insights—both strategic and tactical—that helped me set my team and company on a new course. Having the heart and mind of Charlotte captured in a book is a gift. I'm excited to keep learning from her through reading *The Customer Communication Formula*."

SHANI DOWELL
Possip
Founder and CEO
Tennessee
www.possip.com

"Charlotte taught a virtual class for an association of organizing professionals I belong to. Her class was chock-full of valuable and ready-to-apply information. I remember her professional and thorough way of presenting the class. Relatable in her speaking, she showed expertise on communicating with customers. In her work, she demonstrates strategies that help to create better communication bridges with every single client. I endorse *The Customer Communication Formula* because it will help every single person who reads it—including me."

NACHO EGUIARTE, CPO®
Certified Professional Organizer Specialist
in Chronic Disorganization, Hoarding, and Aging
Owner of nachOrganiza
Serving the cities of Guadalajara and Culiacan in Mexico
www.nachorganiza.com

"I look forward to reading *The Customer Communication Formula* and know I will learn from it. I admire Charlotte's ability to listen and the artful way that she practices what she teaches about Customer Service. The CFOs in our organization continue to be inspired by her presentation, 'Leadership and the CFO.' Charlotte makes a compelling case for working effectively with your internal *and* external customers."

BRIDGET LEE-YOUNG
Chief Executive Officer, Salus Solutions LLC
Chairman of the Board, RTP CFO Forum
North Carolina

"Effective communication is one of the most important business skills required for success. With Charlotte's help, I've learned how to communicate good news, bad news, and unwanted news to various stakeholders globally. I've also learned important lessons about the power of the words we use when communicating with others. The lessons learned have given me greater impact and increased my relationship capital, both personally and professionally. I look forward to reading *The Customer Communication Formula* so I can continue to learn important lessons from Charlotte."

TAMIKA TYSON
Global credit leader
Texas

THE CUSTOMER COMMUNICATION FORMULA

How to communicate with your customers and boost your customer service brand

Charlotte Purvis

WRITEWAY
PUBLISHING

RALEIGH, NORTH CAROLINA

Printed in the United States of America
ISBN 978-1-946425-68-3 (softcover)
ISBN 978-1-946425-81-2 (hardcover)

WRITEWAY
PUBLISHING
www.writewaypublishing.com

To my loving and supportive family,
with gratitude for our special formula:

Courtesy. Communication. Collaboration.

⁓

To my large and loving extended families
for all of your encouragement over the years:

The Curry Family
The Polk Family
The Harris Family
The Gandy Family
The Hinton Family
The Austin Family
The Purvis Family

⁓

CONTENTS

FOREWORD

I met Charlotte when she was an early career professional in a training role for the North Carolina Department of Human Resources. She was asked to help develop an innovative remote training program for child care professionals using teleconferencing through a federally funded research grant. My involvement in the project was to provide expertise in media and communication through a collaboration with the North Carolina Department of Public Instruction (DPI).

Charlotte developed and perfected a special set of communication and remote teaching skills, which led to her starting a successful consulting business. Her timing was impeccable as the Research Triangle Park area of North Carolina was exploding with high-tech companies and a demand for high-touch skills.

During this time, Charlotte and I continued our friendship by meeting for lunch on the Martin Luther King holiday to catch up on our careers. During our luncheon on January 16, 2017, after all these years, I told her that it was time to write a book about what she has learned and perfected for customer service. *The Customer Communication Formula* is now a reality, and it is well worth the wait.

Friendly, Formal, and Focused are the 3-F's of success for achieving a satisfying solution for all customers. The formula in this book is a guide that should be on every Customer Service Professional's desk because it reinforces good manners and good business.

The Customer Communication Formula is a guide for today and the future. My hope is that all generations in the workplace will benefit from the 3-F Formula. As a former educator, I highly recommend this book to high school and college students to provide them with a head start as they transition into the workplace.

I'm delighted that through this book, you will have the opportunity to "meet" Charlotte. You'll understand why she's one of my favorite people. It's an honor to be her mentor and a pleasure and a privilege to be her friend.

As Dr. Martin Luther King said, "The time is always right to do what is right." Three years after our conversation, the right time has arrived! I will refer to this book often and so will you. *The Customer Communication Formula* will not be a bookshelf book; it will be a book to keep on your desk as an indispensable reference.

MARGARET EVANS GAYLE
Consultant
North Carolina

ACKNOWLEDGMENTS

CONTENT ADVISORS
Meghan Young
Paul Irving
Katie Cole

BRANDING CONSULTANT
Meghan Young

EDITING + BOOK AND COVER DESIGN
Lee Heinrich
Charlotte Sinclaire
Melinda Martin
Grace Williamson

BOOK LAUNCH
Daniel Marzullo
Grace Williamson

BUSINESS MANAGER
Sherry Hill

BUSINESS DEVELOPMENT
Iverson Gandy Jr.
Iverson Gandy III

PHOTOS
Michael and Carolyn Kerr

THE HEROES
Customer Service Professionals who contribute to customers,
their organizations, their communities, the world

INTRODUCTION

Friendly, Formal, and Focused. These three words have been the foundation for my entire career as a consultant, trainer, coach, speaker, and Customer Service Enthusiast.

Here's the story that started everything. One of my clients wanted to establish what was to become a best-in-class contact center. They had the best equipment, great furniture (good chairs are important), solid processes, and outstanding leadership. So why were they calling me?

The client had one big concern: how their Customer Service Professionals communicated with customers. I remember what they said as clearly as if the conversation happened yesterday. The client did not want the people answering the phones to sound like they were just sitting around at home talking to their family or chatting with friends.

That is about as straightforward, down-to-earth, and reasonable an expectation as any I've heard in all the years since. So that became my responsibility, to help them create an environment where Customer Service Professionals (CSPs) spoke in a manner that customers would know they were contacting a best-in-class contact center, instead of someone sitting at home chatting on the phone with their family and friends.

My client's vision statement struck me as unique and uncluttered, so it's only fitting that my solution would match their statement in its simplicity. I developed this formula called the 3-F Customer Communication Formula. Top quality customer communication is:

Friendly + Formal + Focused

As simple and straightforward as this sounds now, it took years to develop, test, and refine a formula that is easy to remember, easy to follow, and easy to adapt across channels.

I've since coached and trained hundreds of Customer Service Professionals using my 3-F Customer Communication Formula. And as a result, literally millions of customers have benefited from the service they've received based on my formula.

I will use the term Customer Service Professional (CSP) for those who provide direct services to customers and those who work on behalf of customers in any type of customer service setting.

As a consultant, I quickly learned that the title for CSPs varied across companies and organizations:

• Advisor	• Consultant
• Advocate	• Coordinator
• Agent	• Manager
• Ambassador	• Representative
• Assistant	• Specialist

While I was writing this book, I learned about another title I had not heard before: Customer Service Hero.

I decided to use "Customer Service Professional" (CSP) for these "essential employees" (so I'm not required to select just one title from among the many titles in my client organizations). My great hope is that all CSPs will be given respect and recognition, no matter what title they have.

How did this book come about?

When I go into a company to train CSPs, the company decides what training program makes the most sense given their goals and the company culture. Often, I work with just one person who is selected for my training and coaching program. In other organizations, I work with the entire team of Customer Service Professionals. These CSPs may move on to new roles, new organizations, or new opportunities, sometimes including new leadership roles. But they continue to use the 3-F's whenever they interact with customers, with their colleagues, and even in their personal lives.

> *The practices and tools I have learned*
> *from Ms. Charlotte are truly effective.*
> *They work well on the job and outside of work.*
> TANGELA
> Customer Service Professional
> North Carolina

I've had this book idea in mind for a while. Plus, my clients and colleagues have asked me time and time again to write a book.

Well, the time needed to be right. I knew I wanted to wait until I was absolutely sure the 3-F Formula worked; until I had the time to get all my notes organized; and until I knew my schedule would allow me to commit to getting the writing done.

That opportunity presented itself in the form of the 2020 COVID-19 pandemic. Yes, as I watched the world around us come to a screeching halt, I found myself reflecting on my career, and the words started to flow. Certainly, the global crisis opened my eyes about the critical role Customer Service Professionals play.

I watched as companies faced an increase in customer calls and scrambled to hire more CSPs—who were now working remotely—without having time to provide proper training. I also realized that the need for strong customer service leadership isn't going away after the crisis has passed. So, I decided *now* is the right time to present my 3-F Formula and help CSPs and customer service leaders as they learn to navigate this new world we're stepping into. The best part is that if you use the formula, not only will you be equipped with the training and development programs needed to navigate our "new normal" you'll be set up to take your organization to the next level.

In a world that is becoming increasingly more competitive, when anyone can start a business with a website and a product idea, and when more customers are buying online than ever before, outstanding customer service will set you apart from your competition. There is no question that investing in improving customer service will pay dividends in the long term. So, I ask you this question:

Would you or your company be an ideal client for the Customer Communication Formula?

As I wrote this book, I was thinking of you as a new "virtual" client. As my client, you will implement the formula and you may even share the formula in your organization and ultimately your customers will benefit.

My goal is to "talk to you" just as I do with all of the Awesome Clients I've had the privilege of serving one-to-one over the years. They will tell you that a hallmark of my brand is being interactive. I don't lecture. We have conversations. We connect personally and professionally. You are an ideal client if you appreciate being fully engaged in this process and are open to a new approach that requires self-awareness, attention to detail, and a desire to excel in customer service delivery. And like My Awesome Clients, you will learn that the formula benefits you both personally and professionally.

This book is for you:
- ☐ My Awesome Clients
- ☐ Contact Center team members and leaders:
  - – Customer Service Professionals
  - – Managers, Supervisors, Leaders
  - – Quality Assurance (QA)
  - – Subject Matter Experts (SMEs)
  - – Trainers
- ☐ Corporate Leaders responsible for Customer Care
- ☐ Small Business Owners
- ☐ Faith Community Leaders
- ☐ College and University Leaders
- ☐ College Students
- ☐ K-12 Educators
- ☐ Governmental Agencies
- ☐ Nonprofit and Community Organizations
- ☐ Anyone interested in Customer Service delivery and customer communication

Here's what you will learn and experience while reading *The Customer Communication Formula*:

Chapter 1: It is my pleasure to share the *3-F Formula* so that you will learn the three key words I have introduced to Customer Service Professionals and contact center leaders for over two decades—and that have been used with millions of customers.

Chapters 2, 3, and 4: We review the three *Phases* of interacting with customers—Connection, Conversation, and Closure—and how to apply the 3-F Formula to each phase. In these chapters, you'll learn to speak the language of customer service, manage challenging situations, and offer each customer an excellent experience from Connection through Closure.

Chapter 5: In this chapter, leaders are invited to participate in a self-guided *Consultation*, working through 12 questions focused on brand, leadership, and company culture. (CSPs will find value in this chapter and the next and are invited to read them as well.)

Chapter 6: The self-guided *Consultation* continues with 10 Customer Service Statements Every Organization Needs to develop a custom approach to Customer Service.

Chapter 7: *Extreme Customer Service* is all about delivering great customer service during a crisis and was written while supporting my clients as they managed during the pandemic in 2020. The chapter is dedicated to the Customer Service Professionals on the frontlines during this global crisis.

Chapter 8: This is a bonus chapter on the topic of quality assurance. The chapter is based on a conversation with Jeffrey Newman, Manager, Customer Care, Porsche Cars North America, Inc. We begin with a discussion about the book Jeffrey is writing, *Quality Quality*. You will learn who Jeffrey is, what he does, and his leadership philosophy. He shares some famous "Newmanisms" and gives us a glimpse into what he sees next for Customer Care.

Chapter 9: My clients have great stories to share about how they use the formula in their personal and professional lives. Teams that I've partnered with continue to report how the formula helped them reach and exceed their goals. In this chapter, I share two client success stories that will inspire you. I also share a story about a company I do business with, speaking from my point of view as a Customer Service Enthusiast.

Chapter 10: Speaking of being a Customer Service Enthusiast, in "The Formula and Me," I tell you my story about my passion for Customer Service, how it all started, influences from my beloved Tuscaloosa, Alabama, what I enjoy about being a customer, and the special place in my heart for hotel housekeepers. I also tell you what's next for me after publishing this book.

I have included "Training Talk" features throughout the book where I speak directly to leaders with training responsibility. This feature provides information and insights that you may use for your training programs, meetings, and one-to-one conversations. CSPs, especially those who are invested in their own professional development, will also benefit from reading these sections.

Finally, for readers of this book, I've included exclusive content taken from the notebooks I use with my clients. These "From My Notebook" sections give you a window into my mindset and access to information I have compiled through the years. They will guide you as you think about how to implement the 3-F's.

For you Customer Service Professionals and leaders, the most important point I can get across is that when customers contact you, they want to be treated as human beings by other human beings. The "From My Notebook" sections will help you infuse all of your interactions with this sense of humanity.

You will quickly notice that my approach to customer service is "people first." This means we spend a lot of time looking at the world through the eyes of our customers. In order to be successful in Customer Service, it's important to understand the meaning of the second word: Service. Service means to help, to assist, to listen, to provide support, to contribute to the welfare of others.

CUSTOMER *SERVICE* DOESN'T WORK
WITHOUT A COMMITMENT TO BEING OF *SERVICE.*

Thank you for investing in your professional development and for your interest in delivering best-in-class customer service. Now, let's take a deep dive into the 3-F Formula.

PART ONE

THE CUSTOMER COMMUNICATION FORMULA

CHAPTER 1

THE 3-F CUSTOMER
COMMUNICATION FORMULA
Friendly + Formal + Focused

It's really true. I built my Customer Service consulting business on these three words:

- Friendly
- Formal
- Focused

Of course, these three words aren't entirely self-explanatory. To explain further, I add three more words when I conduct training with clients:

- Friendly
  tone
- Formal
  words
- Focused
  conversation

Taken together, this is the winning formula to guide CSPs and leaders as they interact with customers. I'm delighted that you will now have the opportunity to implement the 3-F Formula in your organization not only for the benefit of your customers but also for your own professional development. Let's get started with a basic discussion about formulas.

A FORMULA

Generally speaking, a formula is a fixed pattern that is used to achieve consistent results. It might be made up of words, numbers, or ideas.

These concepts taken together define a procedure that when followed leads to a desired outcome. In short, formulas are the patterns we follow in life. From driving a car to closing a business deal, no matter what activity you undertake, you follow some type of formula. Communicating with customers in Customer Service is no different. So that's why I call this the 3-F Customer Communication Formula. It is a pattern that you can follow when great customer service is your desired outcome.

The quality of a formula is revealed by its consistency in delivering the outcome you are seeking. A formula that only delivers 50 percent of the time, for instance, needs improvement. For this reason, I wanted to be confident in the results before I presented my formula to Customer Service Professionals.

There are three main characteristics that define a quality formula. Quality formulas are simple, easy to remember, and have been tested for success. The 3-F Formula has these characteristics: it's simple—based on three simple words; it's easy to remember because all of the words start with the same letter; and it has been used by hundreds of Customer Service Professionals in multiple contact centers with millions of customers with great success.

Consider what delivering customer service looks like for your organization. Are you like my client who didn't want their CSPs to sound like they are talking on the phone with their family and friends? Whatever your specific vision, my 3-F Formula will help you get there.

Pause for just a moment and think of a great customer service experience you've had. What do you think made that call, live chat, or other interaction stand out in your mind? Take some time to reflect on your experience.

I'm no mind reader, but I'm willing to guess that what you remember about the experience is based on how the CSP made you feel. Their tone was likely professional, but friendly. And the person you spoke with probably resolved your issue in a way that made you feel heard. Is that correct?

Great customer service experiences strike a delicate balance represented by my 3-F Formula components: Friendly tone, Formal words, and Focused conversation.

So how do you achieve this? Let's start with Friendly.

1. Friendly Tone

In the early stages of developing my formula, when I mentioned the importance of using formal words in delivering customer service, clients often raised concerns about how to keep the communication friendly rather than scripted and stodgy.

By contrast, my concern was the informality. Then I had an aha moment: *keep the friendliness in the tone, not the words.*

In other words, my response to concerns about CSPs using language that is too formal is that we will do all we can to keep the friendliness. This is one reason Friendly comes first in my formula. The selling point is that friendliness is displayed in the tone of voice.

Another reason I start with the tone of voice is because customers tend to hear or experience tone before words—regardless of your delivery channel.

Tone is important because that's what we, as customers and as human beings, use to help us determine the authenticity of the message and the thoughts behind the words.

THE TONE OF VOICE "SETS THE TONE" FOR YOUR CUSTOMER SERVICE. (AND YES, PEOPLE CAN DETECT "TONE" IN WRITTEN MESSAGES TOO.)

During training, I demonstrate this aloud with CSPs. I use a down-beat, disinterested tone to share a message like this:

> *I really enjoy conducting training for all of you. You're a great group of professionals, and I'm so proud to know that you're doing such an outstanding job incorporating all the new lessons about customer service. Congratulations.*

As you can imagine, when they hear this, they don't believe that I am enthusiastic about my time with them—based on the tone. Quickly the Customer Service Professionals in my program learn an important lesson. If the tone and words don't match, *tone typically wins.*

Discussing tone of voice during training, coaching, and calibration often comes with specific challenges such as:

- Evaluation of tone can be subjective since what one person considers friendly another might consider not friendly enough or overly friendly.

- Tone expectations vary from region to region or from country to country.

- Tone is often closely tied to personality and expressing a friendly tone may be easier for some than others.

- Tone may vary depending on how people "feel" at the moment.

- The expectation is that tone may need to change within a conversation, depending on what is being discussed at the time.

TRAINING TALK

FRIENDLY TONE: RECORDED EXAMPLES

In my experience, the best way to meet the challenge of finding the right tone is to provide your team with examples that best match your brand. It also helps to provide your team with examples of the tone of voice you *don't* want associated with your brand. Hearing these various tone examples will be helpful both for new and experienced team members. I recommend creating recordings using internal talent or professional voice actors. These recordings will make it easier to train, coach, and evaluate tone.

While friendliness is all about tone of voice, what we do with our facial expressions also makes a difference. Did you know you can lift your mood by simply smiling at yourself in the mirror? It's true. So, we shouldn't be surprised that when we smile, our facial expressions are reflected in our tone of voice.

Paula Niedenthal, a psychology professor at the University of Wisconsin-Madison (which happens to be my alma mater), found that by using different combinations of facial muscles, human beings actually have different types of smiles.[1] The good news for customer service over the phone is that almost any smile will translate to a friendly tone.

After talking with many CSPs over the years, I find myself using a broader term than "smile" in my training these days. I refer to having an *expressive face*. And the results have been positive.

---

1. Libby Plummer, "There are three types of smile—reward, affiliation, and dominance..." https://www.wired.co.uk/article/smile-study.

Some people just don't resonate with the concept of smiling all day. It can make them feel as if they are being "fake." From the customer perspective, the main issue is for CSPs to sound friendly, project a welcoming tone, and speak with inflection in their voices. For some CSPs this will mean smiling. For others it will mean having a more expressive face. The ultimate test is the customer experience.

FROM MY NOTEBOOK

WRITTEN NOTE USING THE 3-F'S

I had a meeting with Alex (someone I do business with) and within days received a "thank you" note—a handwritten one at that. I am confident that I don't represent this person's largest account. Yet you'd never know that by the level of customer service I receive. This gesture assured me I was not a number. As you would probably guess, I'm still doing business with him and look forward to doing even more.

Following is the note I received, shared with Alex's permission. The note represents the 3-F Formula in every way. He uses a *friendly* tone. It's business-like (*formal*). It's *focused* on me as the client.

> Charlotte,
>
> It was great meeting you last week. I appreciate your time and truly enjoyed hearing about the great work you and your company are doing. I look forward to working with you and continuing to watch the positive impact you have on the community.
>
> Sincerely,
> Alex

Charlotte,

It was great meeting you last week. I appreciate your time and truly enjoyed hearing about the great work you and your company are doing. I look forward to working with you and continuing to watch the positive impact you have on the community.

Sincerely,
Alex

2. Formal Words

As we have discussed, the 3-F Formula begins with a friendly tone. Customers hear or experience the tone before the words. You set the tone for the customer with the goal to make sure the tone is friendly, welcoming, and respectful, implementing the second F, Formal, for the words used.

I've noticed in my years as a Customer Service Consultant that sometimes we try to express our friendliness with our words and the result is too informal. An example is the greeting, "Hey, how ya' doing today?" The challenge is to infuse customer conversations with an appropriate level of formality and professionalism without discounting the friendliness.

One of the most insightful conversations I have ever had with a Customer Service Professional was around this issue of friendly versus formal. This CSP announced to me with great conviction that she preferred to "just be herself" when she delivered customer service. She went on to say that she's a down-home person who doesn't believe in all that "fancy talking." After listening with great interest because she was so passionate and it was clear to me that she was a dedicated Customer Service Professional, I gave this some deep thought.

I realized the issue comes down to one of consistency and fairness.

If this CSP gets to "be herself," then in the interest of fairness—one of my core values—everyone else gets to be themselves too. Now, imagine what that would be like from the point of view of the customer. Suppose we were cooks in a restaurant and each one of us had our own way of making the lunch special. Customers would have no idea what to expect when they ordered the lunch special. Or consider what this policy would mean in a factory where the employees were manufacturing life-saving ventilators. Strict policies and procedures are to be followed consistently to provide for the health and safety of customers. While the policies and procedures in a contact center are not the same as those for manufacturing, consistency and fairness are still key to offering best-in-class customer service.

I had another conversation with the CSP and made my appeal. I reminded her that I was from Alabama and at heart, I am a "down-home person" too. If she gets to be herself, then so would I. And by the time I add all my Alabama terms of endearment, the HR team would stay up at night trying to figure out what to do about me.

This appeal got her attention. Then she said, "Do it for me." Meaning, let her hear how I would speak in my "down-home" voice—the voice I use when talking to my family members and friends back home—how I sound when speaking with people of my parents' generation. So, right there in her cubicle, I literally put on a show for her. I told her how I would manage a call if I was just "being myself." I used multiple terms of endearment, doses and doses of caring and concern, and enough personal talk to make the quality team dizzy.

My family of origin certainly encouraged the "caring and sharing" approach to conversations. And I would think something was wrong if my dear friends and classmates from home didn't add a dose or two in our conversations. But the point stands. There is an important difference between the way we talk to our family and friends and the appropriate way to talk with customers, clients, and business partners.

Fast forward to the next time I saw this CSP. She was proud to share that she had rethought her position and made a change to using more formal words with customers. Our conversation resonated with her, and she enjoyed getting to know me in a new way. Yes, it would be quite "convenient" for Customer Service Professionals to just be themselves. However, that's not an option from the perspective of quality customer service.

Here's another example. When I contacted a company about a computer issue, I had the pleasure of speaking with a very friendly Customer Service Professional. Friendly in tone, friendly in words—well, a totally friendly approach. When I shared my ZIP code, the CSP's conversation went something like this:

> *Now, your ZIP code, what is it?*
> *Funny you should mention that.*
> *I know exactly where that area is!*
> *I have family in that same ZIP code!*
> [Proceeded to share personal details]

One of the big lessons I've learned is that typically situations like this don't happen in isolation. Show me a totally informal interaction like this one and surely multiple others, often more concerning, are just a few clicks away on the call monitoring system.

And in this case, my prediction came true. Later in the conversation, the CSP with a family member living in my ZIP code started singing a song—not humming the song—singing. I don't recall that ever happening before when I was the customer. I've heard humming, yes. But singing? No.

Being the music fan that I am, I asked about the song and that led to yet another off-topic conversation. I learned a lot about the CSP, and I actually didn't mind the conversation because I enjoy observing all types of customer service in action. However, if I were in training mode, I would have explained why this level of informality is not preferred.

Then, I had another aha moment. The CSP knew the call was being recorded. Somewhere along the way, this CSP has likely gotten the message that this level of informality is okay with the Customer Service leaders. The big point here is that this is a leadership issue. When situations like this happen, I look to the leaders, *not the CSPs* for answers.

> *Is the customer service delivery, leadership, coaching, and modeling in your organization sending the message that this level of informality and unprofessionalism is acceptable?*

Here's what I've been waiting to share and I'll rest my case about the singing CSP with a family member in my ZIP code. *I learned that this CSP is a leader in that organization.* Full stop.

 **FROM MY NOTEBOOK**

INFORMALITY LEADS TO MORE INFORMALITY

I had been away from one of my clients for a while due to some business transitions. I was pleased when it was time to go back and continue my Customer Service programs.

When I was there previously, we trained CSPs to use this phrase: *May I have your Social Security Number?*

By the time I returned, the phrase had been shortened to the quite informal: *May I have your Social?*

One of the lessons that I share with clients is that informality leads to more informality. So I warned them that if they've moved from "Social Security Number" to "Social," it was only a matter of time before CSPs would start to say, *"May I have your Sosh?"*

This was several years ago, yet I still remember the response. The CSPs in another one of their contact centers had already started using "Sosh."

I used the 3-F Formula and my influence to persuade the client to continue using the more formal and appropriate "Social Security Number."

3. Focused Conversation

This aspect of the formula has required testing and more testing to get it right. Simply put, the customer call or interaction ideally has a *distinct* beginning, middle, and end. It was only recently that I began using this alliterative list to further define the final F, Focused, in three phases:

• Connection   • Conversation   • Closure

When I join a calibration session, where I sit down with leaders, listen to some recorded calls, and hear a CSP move from one phase of a focused conversation to the next with ease, it's like listening to good music or an engaging story. The CSP is always one step ahead—welcoming, listening, managing, anticipating, and delighting the customer. My rave reviews are just that, and I enjoy sending personal notes to CSPs with compliments about how well they manage their calls.

ADVANCED CUSTOMER SERVICE PROFESSIONALS DON'T JUST "TAKE CALLS," THEY MANAGE THEM WITH SKILL AND WITH STYLE.

FROM MY NOTEBOOK

WHO'S MANAGING THE CALL? THE CSP? THE CUSTOMER?

1. Who sets the tone?
2. Who projects confidence?
3. Who decides what's next?

4. Who mentions solutions?
5. Who initiates closure?
6. Who does the follow-up?

It all begins with an awareness of the importance of call flow from the customer's perspective. Customers are delighted when we can welcome them, listen to learn the purpose of their call, guide them to a solution, and close with a recap and appreciation. That's what I call focused conversation—not just being focused during the conversation but being focused on the customer and their experience.

TESTING THE FORMULA

The 3-F Formula has been put to the test for over two decades with these groups:

- Contact center leaders
- Customer Service Professionals (CSPs)
- CSP teams in pharmaceutical companies
- Clients seeking one-to-one communication coaching
- Customers (by the millions)

The principles of the 3-F Formula have been shared with these and other groups for presentations and training purposes:

- Church staff
- Corporate leaders
- Corporate teams

- College faculty and staff
- College students
- Community leaders

The formula has withstood all the testing and produced the desired results for clients and their customers.

The next question is: How can you apply the 3-F Formula to your calls and other customer interactions? Let's get practical and tactical as we continue with the next chapter: The Connection Phase.

CHAPTER 2

THE CONNECTION PHASE

When I talk about giving your customers an experience that transforms them into loyal customers who rave about you, I'm talking about a customer service experience that uses the 3-F Formula and flows from connection to conversation to closure. In this and the following two chapters, let's consider each of these phases in detail.

We all understand the importance of starting our day right, opening a speech right, or "getting off on the right foot" in a relationship. The lessons about starting right and making a good first impression also apply to customer service.

After observing thousands of customer interactions, I can now predict the outcome of most calls by listening to the way they start out. CSPs who pay attention to key details during the greeting and opening are more likely to pay attention throughout the communication with the customer.

A great start can set you up for success and give you an anchor if things get off track.

A not-so-great start can set you up for a not-so-great finish with little to "fall back on" later.

BEFORE THE CONNECTION

Consider the following five attributes in preparation for the call. Do a quick check-in by asking yourself the questions associated with each attribute:

Clarity
What is our mission? What are the expectations for each customer interaction? What are our values?

Compartmentalize
Am I able to detach myself from personal life issues during this customer interaction?

Composure
Even before I answer, will I prepare myself by smiling or having an expressive face?

Consistency
Will I provide the same high level of customer service during this interaction as though it is my first of the day?

Customer-focus
Am I ready to focus *exclusively* on this customer?

THE GREETING

Hi, and thanks for calling us.
So what can I do for you today?
Okay, go ahead and give me your name.
Got it.
How 'boutchore telephone number?
Let's go ahead and get that from you.
Now, your ZIP code, what is it?
Funny you should mention that ZIP code.
I know exactly where that area is!
Someone dear to me lives near there.
That's because of a special situation...

This is a composite of some openers I've heard as a Customer Service Consultant and that I experienced as a customer. This is a classic example of how CSPs can sound without the 3-F Formula. First, the opening is too friendly. Second, the words are informal. And third, the conversation is not focused. This is an example of what my clients don't want their CSPs to sound like.

This first impression is key to setting the tone for the call or inter-action. Remember, the impression comes across through words and tone. Getting the first impression right is often a challenge for CSPs due to lack of clarity around expectations, the repetitiveness of managing calls and other customer interactions, and the anxiety of not knowing what is going to happen when they engage with a particular customer.

CSPs can learn to use their words and their tone to provide a "grand opening." The following table gives you suggestions to convey your intended message.

Use these words plus a friendly tone	To convey this message to the customer
Thank you for calling [organization name].	We are pleased that you contacted us. It is my pleasure to be of service to you.
My name is [first name].	I am responsible. I am accountable.
How may I assist you? How may I help you?	I am prepared to assist you. This interaction is all about you, our valued customer.

Note that these are examples for your consideration. Your organization might prefer to use different verbiage.

TRANSITION STATEMENTS AND ADVANCED TRANSITION STATEMENTS

Transition statements are used to confirm that the customer has been heard and that the CSP is ready to be of service and find solutions. I'm a big advocate of transition statements and what I call advanced transition statements because:

- They require that CSPs really listen to understand the purpose of the call.
- They give the customer the opportunity to clarify the purpose of the call, if needed.
- They serve as a transition to the next step, seeking solutions.
- When they are used, it prevents the interaction from becoming purely "transactional."
- They serve as an "agreement" between the customer and the CSP about what they will focus on.

Transition statements
- I'll be happy to help you.
- It will be my pleasure to assist you.
- Yes, I'm able to assist you.

Advanced transition statements use the customer's own words to confirm that the CSP is clear about the reason for the call or for the contact.

Advanced transition statements:
- I'll be happy to help you with your question *about the coupon*.
- It will be my pleasure to assist you *with your password*.
- Yes, I am able to assist you *with your account information*.

REQUESTING CUSTOMER INFORMATION

Next, the CSP typically will start collecting information to protect the person's privacy, to document the call, to access the person's information, or to add the person's information to the database. During the early years in my consulting career, a CSP would be expected to say something like this after the transition statement:

> *May I have your name please?*
> *May I have your address?*
> *May I have your telephone number?*
> *Please confirm the last four digits of your Social Security Number (or account number).*
> *Thank you.*

Over time, I've thought this through and suggested ways to take the clutter out of the customer communication.

Now, the recommendation is to use this approach:

May I have your name please?
And your address?
And your telephone number?
Finally, please confirm the last four digits of your Social
*   Security Number (or account number).*
Thank you.

Sometimes the above approach won't work because the customer wants to take the CSP in a different direction. For example, the customer might begin with a list of issues. Here's an example and two possible CSP responses.

CSP: *Thank you for calling the Very Best Company. My name is [name]. How may I assist you?*
CUSTOMER: *I am calling because I have a serious problem plus I'm worried about another situation and it's just been hard to get through to y'all... and I have been waiting for over 30 minutes.*
CSP: *Okay go ahead and give me your name.*

In this response:

- No transition statement is used.
- There's no acknowledgement of the customer's situation and the hold time.
- The response does not indicate that the customer was heard.
- There's use of commanding language ("go ahead and give me...").

An opening like this is generally a predictor of an outcome that does not meet expectations.

This is an opportunity for active listening. Here is what the CSP could say to improve the previous response:

I apologize for your wait time. Thank you for your patience.
I'm happy to help you with your question about your
special situation and any other issues.
In order to better assist you, typically we begin with a
few questions.
May I have your name please?
And your address?
And your telephone number?
Finally, please confirm the last four digits of your Social
Security Number (or account number).
Thank you.

Alternatively, the CSP might want to expand their lead-in by saying something like "In order to best assist you, let's begin with some questions to protect your privacy."

FROM MY NOTEBOOK

MAY I HAVE YOUR TELEPHONE NUMBER...?

Here's a line that I've heard some CSPs use that really got my attention: "May I have your telephone number in case we get disconnected?"

My recommendation is to omit "in case we get disconnected." This is the beginning of the call, the Connection Phase, and already the CSP is mentioning a potential problem and drawing attention to the technology. Imagine what the customer is thinking at this moment.

Typically, it is sufficient to ask for the telephone number without the mention of the potential disconnect and then record and use the number as appropriate.

FROM MY NOTEBOOK

FOCUS ON THE CUSTOMER: PREFERRED PHRASES

Customers want to be seen as individuals, not tickets or cases. Here are phrases to avoid because they focus on your internal process and some preferred phrases that focus on the customer.

Phrases to avoid	Preferred phrases
I'm going to pull you up in the system.	I am accessing your contact information.
I need to find you in the system.	I am accessing the information now.
I'm trying to find you in the database.	I am accessing your file.
Now, I see you in our database.	I am accessing your previous contacts with us.
Bear with me while I find you in the system.	I am accessing the notes from your call yesterday.

Note that these are examples for your consideration. Your organization might prefer to use different verbiage.

TREATING CUSTOMERS LIKE PEOPLE

According to the Executive Summary in the 2019 Gladly Customer Expectations Report, 69% of customers surveyed feel they're treated like a ticket, not a person.

Customer's Name

One way to make customers feel that they are being treated as people and not tickets is to use their names.

Here's what I recommend. Use the name as soon as you hear it. This helps you to confirm the name, confirm the correct pronunciation, and make a connection with the customer.

Here's what you want to avoid:

- Not using the name at all during the call, missing the opportunity to connect with the customer

- Using the name excessively, which may be perceived as condescending and authoritative

- Mispronouncing the name during the close, missing the opportunity to confirm the correct pronunciation

- Using the wrong name during the close, making the customer wonder if we are paying attention or if they are just a ticket

Courtesy and Professional Titles

I encourage you to have a conversation about the use of courtesy titles and professional titles such as ma'am, sir, Ms., Mr., or Dr. for instance. It has been my practice to avoid making this a "one size fits all" discussion (even though I have my personal preferences).

Within each organization, the decision is usually based on one of three factors:

- Organizational culture
- Regional practices
- Personal preferences

As your consultant, I will share some insights with you:

- Please don't leave this decision to personal preference. Try having this conversation with people from different regions, different generations, and different cultural backgrounds. You'll likely learn there are some deep-rooted opinions about the use of courtesy and professional titles.

- When in doubt, start with the most formal: Ms., Mr., or Dr. I find it a bit awkward to listen to a call when the customer's first name is used and due to the customer's generation or preference, the customer then makes a correction. I highly recommend a training program on communicating across generations—not just about the titles to use but about other expectations as well. The expectations will vary from country to country, from region to region. I look forward to learning more about how my readers and clients address this topic.

- I've also observed those awkward moments where the CSP uses "Mr." only to learn they're speaking to a "Ms." or vice versa. Two considerations here: First, be aware that this can happen and try to avoid this mix up. Be prepared to apologize, make a quick correction, and move forward.

Courtesy Phrases

I received an email from a company I do business with and my immediate reaction was to share this with my readers. This is an example of a customer communication with no courtesy phrases. (I've changed the wording a bit so as not to disclose the source and specific topic.) File this under lack of courtesy phrases and the use of commanding words:

You need to reach out to the persons who requested your services. They have a process they have to follow. I do not have access to that information. [28 words]

Here's a version with courtesy phrases and a more courteous approach, adding only 11 additional words:

Thank you for your email. Regarding the [information you requested], please contact the persons who originally requested your services. They will be able to submit your request.

If you need additional assistance, please feel free to contact me again. [39 words]

ADDING COURTESY PHRASES WILL HELP TO CREATE A POSITIVE CONNECTION AND CUSTOMER EXPERIENCE.

TRAINING TALK

WHAT TO LISTEN FOR AT THE BEGINNING OF THE CALL

Tone: Was the tone friendly? Did the CSP combine a friendly tone with the use of formal words?

Transitions: Did the CSP use either a transition statement or an advanced transition statement?

Non-Transactional: Was the Customer treated like a "ticket" or shown the proper respect and courtesy with words and tone?

FROM MY NOTEBOOK

5 NOISES TO AVOID WHEN SPEAKING WITH CUSTOMERS

- Coughing (solution: mute button)
- Throat-clearing (solution: mute button)
- Gum chewing (inappropriate)
- Eating (inappropriate)
- Tapping on the desk and related noises (inappropriate)

THE NAME GAME

There is an expectation for CSPs to pronounce names correctly each and every time, including names of:

• People   • Products   • Programs

When speaking with a customer who has a unique name (here, unique means "unique to you"), consider the following:

- Confirm the spelling of the name.
- After confirming the spelling, if you need help with the pronunciation, it's typically okay to ask, "Would you pronounce your first name again, please?"
- A suggestion is to make note of the phonetic spelling (write the name the way it sounds).

After discussing this with CSPs, I've learned that sometimes it is best to forego the use of the customer's name versus mispronouncing it. I recommend that CSPs use a friendly tone along with "you" and "your" throughout the call. This can help CSPs make a personal connection even when they are not able to use the customer's name.

Here is some suggested verbiage:

- Now that **you've** explained the situation, here are two questions for **you**...

- **You** mentioned earlier...

- Thank **you** for sharing **your** feedback...

- What other questions may I answer for **you** about the new product?

- It's been a pleasure to speak with **you** today.

FROM MY NOTEBOOK

UNIQUE NAMES

When conducting client programs, I now ask for the phonetic spelling of unique names. If you have a unique name, a suggestion is to create the phonetic spelling to share as needed. For all of us in Customer Service, a request is to pronounce names correctly and avoid referring to unique names as "hard-to-pronounce" or "foreign."

Pronouncing a person's name correctly demonstrates respect and expresses appreciation for their personhood.

APOLOGIES

You might wonder why I'm bringing this issue up during the first phase. During the Connection Phase, it's important to listen to the customer's words and tone and to address any issues right away rather than later in the call.

In some instances, customers begin the call with a list of issues or complaints and the outcome of the call depends on how well the CSP can diffuse the situation. Sometimes an apology can go a long way toward setting a positive tone for the rest of the call. Common customer issues include:

- Human error
- Miscommunication
- Disappointment
- Anger and frustration
- Technology issues
- Process issues
- Business partner issues
- Issues outside CSP's control
- Company feedback
- Industry feedback

When the customer is speaking about one of these issues, the tendency is to jump in right away or ignore the issue because of the lack of skill in managing these situations. Sometimes CSPs think that by addressing the issue, it's being magnified, so it's best to ignore it. Ignoring the issue demonstrates indifference on the part of the CSP and is likely to create a less-than-positive overall customer experience. It is important to pause and address the issue right away because:

- Even if you want to move on, the customer might be stuck right there—still upset about waiting 30 minutes to speak with you, for instance.

- During the Connection Phase, you have the opportunity to set the tone for the rest of the call. If you ignore the customer issue, you are missing an opportunity to connect, listen actively, and make the customer feel heard.

- You might find that you need to transfer the customer's call to another CSP—you might have missed an opportunity to apologize and the customer might then carry that same disappointment into the next interaction.

So, what is the best way to address these issues? The following tables offer suggestions to use (and some verbiage to avoid).

When the situation calls for	Use phrases like this
Sincere tone, fewer words	My apologies.
An apology on behalf of the organization	Please accept our apologies.
An apology when something unintended happens	We certainly regret you had that experience.
An apology that says let's move forward to a solution	Thank you for telling me about... We apologize for... Here's what I will do. I will...

Avoid phrases like these	For these reasons
I'm sorry.	This makes it all about "us" and as the saying goes, "sorry is a sorry word."
Sorry 'bout that.	This phrase is too informal.
My bad.	This is slang; it's too informal.
Oops. Oopsy.	This is slang; it's too informal.
Wow, we really messed up that time, didn't we?	This is a disparaging remark.
To be honest with you, that area has been having a lot of issues lately.	This is a disparaging remark.

Communication barriers to avoid	Related verbiage to avoid
Defensiveness	We have a good track record, and it's not like we didn't try...
Indifference when customer shares a story or feedback	Oh okay, let me get your name...
Argumentativeness	That's not what we show here, so clearly we didn't do anything wrong.
Blaming	To be honest, I'm not surprised. We've had a lot of issues with that department.
Focusing on self vs. focusing on the customer	I've done everything I can think of to try to make this right for you...

Note that these are examples for your consideration. Your organization might prefer to use different verbiage.

FROM MY NOTEBOOK

WHEN DO WE ALL LOSE?

If you "win" an argument with a customer, we all lose.

In a bit of irony, studies continue to show that recovering well from a "failure" in service can lead to a higher customer satisfaction level. Customers tend to be even more loyal after the CSP (or another representative of the organization) apologizes and a correction is made. This is called the "service recovery paradox," a concept first introduced by Michael McCollough and Sundar G. Bharadwaj.

For example, if your organization encounters a large-scale problem such as a system outage, it's a good idea to step back and consider what your customers are experiencing. By communicating with them clearly, accurately, and in a timely manner, you can reduce their stress and demonstrate that you are concerned about them.[2]

The service recovery paradox alone is a pretty compelling reason for CSPs to apologize in a professional manner during the Connection Phase and throughout the interaction.

EXPRESSIONS OF EMPATHY

Empathy has never been more important.
DALE
Customer Service Professional
California

---

2. Matthew Patterson, ("How to Communicate with Customers During a System Outage,") https://www.helpscout.com/helpu/outage-status-update/.

Invariably, CSPs hear stories from customers where an expression of empathy is the appropriate response. The opportunity to express empathy often comes at the start of the call, during the Connection Phase, because this is the time when customers share their stories. Expressing empathy can be one of the biggest challenges for CSPs.

Here are some of the questions that might arise when discussing the importance of empathy for customer service:

Q. *Is it appropriate to express empathy in a business environment?*

A. Yes, it is—especially with customers. Expressing empathy helps to make human connections and prevents customers from being treated as tickets, numbers, or cases.

Q. *Is there a risk of going overboard and being "too empathetic?"*

A. Yes, there is a risk. Some of the stories we hear push us beyond our training and to a place beyond words. Proper training and practice will help CSPs know what to say and how to say it, so that their expressions of empathy are appropriate.

Q. *What if empathy is interpreted as pity?*

A. Empathy and pity are not the same. Empathy says, "I feel *with* you." Pity says, "I feel sorry *for* you." When CSPs express empathy appropriately, it's as though the CSP and customer are "on the same team."

If the customer feels pitied, it is recommended that the CSP offer an apology (with the appropriate tone). One that comes to mind is, "My apologies, that was not my intent. I have an appreciation for what you shared and am glad you contacted us..."

Q. *What words work best?*

A. The following are suggested phrases to use when expressing empathy:

- I hear you.
- Thank you for sharing your feedback.
- Thank you for telling me about the situation.
- It's important for me to know those details, thank you.
- Yes, I follow what you're saying.
- Your reaction is certainly understandable.
- Absolutely, it's understandable that you feel that way.
- Well, I'm really glad you called. I would be happy to help you with your question.
- You mentioned a concern about the new guidelines, please tell me more...

Q. *What if I, as a CSP, rank low on the empathy (feelings) scale?*

A. The good news here is that the focus in customer service is not so much how the CSP *feels*—it's on the *expression* of empathy. With training, CSPs can develop the skills to express empathy appropriately.

Q. *Can you train people to have empathy?*

A. Yes, CSPs can be trained on the definition of empathy, the importance of empathy, empathy expectations, when to express empathy, and on the appropriate verbiage to use.

TRAINING TALK

EMPATHY AND CUSTOMER SERVICE

Here is a major insight for leaders: We can't tell people how to feel; we can't monitor their feelings; and it's very unlikely that we'll be able to experience consistency among the CSPs in the way they express their feelings. One of my lines is that we can't "legislate feelings." But what we can have is appropriate consistency in expectations, training, and delivery of empathetic expressions.

You are encouraged to offer training and support to help CSPs express empathy. If you would like to make improvements in this area, one idea is to invite a guest presenter with experience in Emotional Intelligence and empathy to train CSPs.

Here are 5 key points about empathy and customer service:

1. Empathy is an expectation for Customer Service.
2. Individual expectations about empathy will vary from customer to customer.
3. Empathy ties into your organization's mission, vision, and values, so it is important to include empathy in Customer Service training.
4. Likewise, it is important to have a consistent approach to the expression of empathy among CSPs.
5. It is important to express empathy to both your external *and* internal customers.

Empathy is considered an essential skill and is typically included on lists of key customer service skills. A recent list from Help Scout, for example, included empathy along with other related skills like patience, attentiveness, and the ability to read customers.[3]

---

3. Gregory Ciotti, "16 Key Customer Service Skills (and How to Develop Them,") https://www.helpscout.com/blog/customer-service-skills/.

Be Kind
FOR MANY OF THE
CUSTOMERS YOU
SPEAK TO ARE
FIGHTING A HARD
Battle

FROM MY NOTEBOOK

THE "NANOSECOND STOP"

One of the top topics that I discuss with CSPs is what I call the "nano-second stop." Listening to interactions between customers and CSPs, I soon noticed instances where the CSP and customer were speaking at the same time. It almost always sounded like an argument or a game to see who would get to speak.

After some testing, I developed a coaching approach to help CSPs address this issue. At first, I suggested that CSPs stop speaking immediately whenever the customer started to speak. Over time, though, I suggested that they stop in a nanosecond—in the middle of a sentence or in the middle of a word (the advanced version). I find the best way to confirm understanding and buy-in is to practice the nanosecond stop.

Start with a demonstration of a talk-over so CSPs can hear how this sounds. Then move to nanosecond demonstrations and practice. Include the advanced version, stopping in the middle of a word.

Some phone systems require the CSPs to pause slightly before speaking to avoid the talk-overs. CSPs are encouraged to practice speaking in a manner that prevents talk-overs.

FROM MY NOTEBOOK

THE SWIVEL

One of my most powerful CSP moments is so memorable that I've given it a name: "The Swivel." I have shared the story with countless clients—leaving many of them speechless.

Here is the story: I was scheduled to conduct a "side-by-side" with a CSP, who was returning from leave. Without going into the details, I'll share the reason with you: The leave was required after the CSP received the phone call that parents hope they never have to answer.

So there I was, side-by-side with someone buried in grief. Thankfully, we already knew each other and had a good business relationship. The "side by side" included call observations to be followed by a coaching session. Before any calls came in, I wanted to know how she was doing. You can imagine the conversation. It was a privilege to listen and to express empathy. Our conversation serves as an example of the importance of expressing empathy to the CSPs, so the CSPs will then be more motivated to express empathy to the customer.

Then, *ring, ring*. A customer called.

Using the 3-F Formula, the CSP answered the call: "Thank you for calling [organization name]. My name is [first name]. How may I help you?"

There was no hint of emotion, no hint that she was in deep grief and had just returned from leave. I am still in a state of admiration watching the transformation from our conversation to the connection with the customer. After the call ended and documentation was completed, she "swiveled" in her chair, and we were back to discussing her grief and pain.

Then, *ring, ring*. Another customer called. Repeat.

It was in that moment that I realized if this CSP could do "The Swivel," then others can too—no matter their personal situation. That to me is what being a CSP is all about. Knowing how to do "The Swivel."

FROM MY NOTEBOOK

STICKY NOTE REMINDERS

Here's one of the simplest ideas I've shared that has had the greatest results. As an example, when CSPs are challenged with the use of "Can I" versus "May I" (which is preferred), I invite them to do this:

Write "Can I" on a sticky note. Cross it out (in red for more emphasis) and post this note so that it's in view during customer interactions. This works with any phrase to avoid.

Results: overwhelmingly positive!

Another idea is to create branded customer service notes for CSPs to help them remember the tips you share. You can also use these notes to congratulate CSPs for a customer service accomplishment.

The Very Best Company
Customer Service
Coaching Program

~~Can I~~
May I

Thank you for all that you do
for our Customers.

How About a Pop-Up Break?

Before you go to the next chapter, how about taking a pop-up break? Consider encouraging your CSPs to take pop-up breaks throughout their day too.

Research shows the value of taking short breaks during your work-day. Here are five reasons why:[4]

- A "movement break," such as taking a short walk in a natural setting, is essential for your physical and emotional health.
- Breaks can prevent "decision fatigue."
- Breaks restore motivation, especially for long-term goals.
- Breaks increase productivity and creativity.
- A "walking break" helps you consolidate memories and improve learning.

Since we've just talked about the benefits of breaks for CSPs, I'll share a story from my notebook that is also important when discussing the health and wellbeing of the CSPs.

FROM MY NOTEBOOK

CHAIRS FOR THE CSPS

You might be surprised to know one of the first things I notice when I walk into a contact center (or if I'm looking at a photo of a work-from-home environment).

---

4. Meg Selig, "How Do Work Breaks Help Your Brain? 5 Surprising Answers," https://www.psychologytoday.com/us/blog/changepower/201704/how-do-work-breaks-help-your-brain-5-surprising-answers.

I notice the chairs. Why? That's where CSPs spend most of their time, and it says a lot when leaders recognize this and make sure they provide the very best options. Having comfortable chairs that allow CSPs to do their jobs better is a contribution to excellent customer service delivery and to the health of CSPs.

Earlier in my career, I had a consulting opportunity in a contact center with chairs that still make me cringe when I think about them. (My colleague on that project says she's still cringing too.) The chairs looked like they had met some hard times and were headed for the trash heap. They didn't match—a clear indication that they were purchased piecemeal with the goal of paying the least amount possible.

Show me some challenged chairs and I'll predict that the chairs are but a symptom of some other underlying issues and an indication of how leaders see the value of CSPs.

I'll fast forward. Those underlying issues I predicted indeed revealed themselves. Later, the center was closed.

We've now completed the Connection Phase—including the greeting, use of transition statements, requesting customer information, using the customer's name along with courtesy phrases, offering apologies, and expressing empathy when appropriate. The interaction now moves to the Conversation Phase. In the next chapter, we explore ways to use the 3-F Formula to help manage the conversation and keep the customer engaged.

CHAPTER 3

THE CONVERSATION PHASE

In this chapter, we'll examine tested and proven ways to manage customer service conversations. We'll also explore techniques for managing challenging situations and how to use the 3-F Formula to do so. Let's acknowledge as we begin that customer service conversations vary widely and on multiple levels.

Conversational variations	Details
Length	Anywhere from a few minutes to over an hour
Complexity	Customers contact you to ask for basic information such as: • a telephone number • hours of operation Or with more complex requests, such as: • to find out about a power outage or other outages • to take care of an urgent need for medication

Conversational variations	Details
Purpose	Reasons a customer may contact a CSP: • to update their address • when they may have just received a life-changing medical diagnosis Or a family member may need to provide an update on the passing of a loved one.
Emotions	Other reasons a customer may contact a CSP: • to compliment a team member • to express irritation about being on hold for a lengthy period • to report great disappointment with a long-standing issue—perhaps not just with your organization, but with your entire industry
Security	CSPs also respond to situations like these: • harassment • threats • inquiries from competitors • fraudulence These typically require legal, security, HR, or management intervention.

Note that these are examples for your consideration. Your organization might prefer to use different verbiage.

This chart only covers some of the variations, as it is impossible to cover them all. I do, however, present some best practices to address the variations in your conversations with customers. All of the best practices listed here have been tested. Plus, they meet the following criteria:

- They are evergreen. They have been used in all—or nearly all—of my client engagements, for over two decades.
- They address the most requested issues. Clients continue to ask for help with these topics.
- They are customer approved. Customers appreciate the approach as indicated by their feedback.

6 BEST PRACTICES FOR THE CONVERSATION PHASE

1. Seeking Solutions

After identifying or clarifying the purpose of the call or contact during the Connection Phase, the CSP is ready to direct the conversation toward a solution and to invite the customer to join them in being solution-focused.

Let's look at some examples of what a customer might consider to be the "problem" and the solution the CSP can begin to focus on.

Customer "problem"	Customer service solution
Trouble using your product	I'll be happy to answer your questions about the product.
Problem with the website	It will be my pleasure to help you access the website so you can find the information you're searching for.
Frustration with the process for submitting an online form	Certainly, I can assist you with submitting the form.
Angry with the company	It's helpful to hear your feedback. We certainly regret that you had that experience. I would like to learn more so I may assist you and share your experience with our manager.

Note that these are examples for your consideration. Your organization might prefer to use different verbiage.

Seeking a solution during this Conversation Phase may take some time. It's important to set expectations so the customer is comfortable with the process. Here are some suggestions:

A. Keep the customer updated about what is being done and the expected amount of time needed. This shows respect for the customer's time and gives the customer an option to continue to hold or request follow-up communication.

FROM MY NOTEBOOK

MAY I PLACE YOUR CALL ON HOLD?

This verbiage has been tested for placing calls on hold:

- May I place your call on hold while I access that information for you?
- May I place your call on a brief hold while I access that information for you?
- May I place your call on a one- to two-minute hold while I access that information for you?
- May I place your call on hold while I consult with my team member about the coupon for you?

We ask for permission to place *calls* on hold rather than telling the customer what we're going to do.

✓ **May I** place your call on hold?
✗ I'm going to place your call on hold.

WE PLACE CALLS ON HOLD, WE DON'T PLACE CALLERS ON HOLD.

B. State customer updates from the customer's point of view, free of internal jargon and without including the "whole story."

BEFORE: Focused on the organization	AFTER: Focused on the customer
Thank you for sharing your information. I have tagged your A-C-M-E form and will escalate that to the A-L-A team. It will go through their reverification process with the GEMS group and within a week, we'll have the final update from the A-E-R for your region.	Thank you for sharing your information. I will forward the form to the team that conducts the reviews and will contact you by Friday the 5th with your update. Would you like for me to call you or send an email?

Note that these are examples for your consideration. Your organization might prefer to use different verbiage.

C. Confirm organizational expectations around the amount of time to leave a customer's call on hold.

According to a recent Genesys Customer Experience survey, on average, consumers say the acceptable length of time to wait to speak with a representative is between one and three minutes.[5]

The guidelines for hold times vary from organization to organization. Once the guidelines are set, it is important for CSPs to know what to do if the hold time exceeds the guideline. Here's an example:

Return from hold, using the customer name and adding "thank you" for holding:

• Ms. Customer?...thank you for holding.

---

5. To view the full report, download here: https://www.genesys.com/resources/genesys-state-of-customer-experience-research.

Offer an apology for the extended hold:

- My apologies for the extended hold time.

State the benefit to the customer and set a new expectation:

- I am still speaking with the verification team about your question.

Confirm that the customer would like the option of continuing to hold:

- Would you like to remain on hold while I...?
- Would you like for me to call you back?
- Would you like to call us back?
- Would you like for us to send the details in an email?

D. Avoid self-talk, singing, humming, and the like while accessing the information. For example:

- Hmm, let me see here...where is that code...I know I've seen it...
- Let me think...I don't know if that coupon is still available.
- Come on computer...don't slow down on me now.
- This is taking too long...this is...hmm...oh there it is...

E. Use your customer communication skills to seek input, gain buy-in, and confirm as needed. Remember, this Conversation Phase is just that, a conversation. Approaching the conversation from this perspective increases the interaction and engagement, which ultimately impacts customer satisfaction.

2. Offering Information

In addition to solving a customer's problem, it is important to be aware of the way in which information is offered during the conversation. In some cases, even if a customer leaves with a solution to their problem, they may be left feeling unsatisfied because of the way in which the information is offered.

Suzanne Schlosberg wrote an article on likeability that I keep in my "evergreen" file. In the article, Schlosberg reviews seven factors that contribute to a person's "likeability." One factor is the use of complete sentences. This is an easily overlooked requirement for communicating with customers.

Schlosberg quotes psychologist Albert Mehrabian, PhD, who says, "The more eloquently you speak, the better you'll be received." Speaking in complete sentences is one path to more eloquence—and such a quick win as you'll see in the examples below.[6]

Notice how using complete sentences in conversations with customers also fulfills the Formal component of the 3-F Formula.

Customer says:	Incomplete and informal responses	Eloquent responses using complete sentences
Is everything going well there for you?	Yep	Yes, everything is going well, thank you.
I'll call you back on Monday.	Sure thing Awesome sauce!	I look forward to speaking with you on Monday.

---

6. Suzanne Schlosberg, "Do You Like Me? Want to Boost Your Popularity? All It Takes is a Few Simple Steps," *Health* Magazine, September 2005.

Customer says:	Incomplete and informal responses	Eloquent responses using complete sentences
May I have your name again?	Madison	Certainly, my name is Madison. Yes, my name is Madison and my last name begins with H. My name is Madison and my ID# is 35401.
What are your business hours?	8 to 6	We're available from 8:00 AM until 6:00 PM Eastern Time, Monday through Saturday.
How do you spell [product name]?	P_r_o_d_u_c_t _n_a_m_e	The product name is spelled p_r_o_d_u_c_t_ n_a_m_e.
Thank you.	No problem You bet!	You're welcome.
Have a nice day.	You too	Thank you. Thank you, and I hope you have a nice day.

Note that these are examples for your consideration. Your organization might prefer to use different verbiage.

TELEPHONE NUMBERS AND DATES

One of the goals in Customer Service is not to have to repeat the information shared with the customer. You want the information to be clear, complete, and delivered with the right pace so that it is easily understood.

When I noticed that CSPs were repeating telephone numbers, I decided to take a closer look and develop a solution for my clients. One solution is to state telephone numbers in groups of 3's and 2's.

Instead of 9191234567, say 919...123...45...67

For vanity numbers, state both the vanity number and the actual number. Example: 1 555 A VANITY and 1...555...282...64...89

This approach is a winner with my clients. And when using this format with the best pace for the customer, customers typically don't need to ask for repeats.

When sharing dates with customers, I suggest CSPs use the formal and complete date. This is especially important when speaking with people who have challenges processing information (temporary or long-term). I'm thinking especially of some patients who call contact centers for pharmaceutical companies.

Let's use July 12, 2021 as an example:

Recommended:
   July twelfth, two thousand twenty-one.

Not recommended:
   Seven twelve twenty-one.

Note: This information may need to be adapted for your country's telephone number format and date format. A suggestion is to develop a format that flows well, test it out, and establish guidelines for these very frequent exchanges in Customer Service.

TRAINING TALK

"C" AS IN CUSTOMER AND "S" AS IN SERVICE

Another technique that comes in handy for customer service is pho-netic spelling. When spelling words and names, match each letter with a word that begins with the same letter to avoid confusion. It is impor-tant to provide standard words to use for this purpose, otherwise, CSPs will choose the word they prefer for each letter of the alphabet, which results in randomness. I've also heard CSPs pause as they search for the best word, which results in wasted time and often the words chosen are not the best choices because:

- The word is not one that the customer would typically use.
- The word has an unintended association.
- The CSP selects a word and then later uses a different word for the same letter.

These words were listed in some of the phonetic spelling charts I found:
- B as in boy
- K as in kilo
- Q as in queen
- W as in whiskey
- Y as in Yankee

For each of these words, I can think of customer service scenarios where they might not be the best choice. I suggest these guidelines for develop-ing a phonetic chart for your organization:
- Seek input from selected CSPs.
- Be thoughtful and intentional when deciding on each word.
  - Is the word likely to be familiar to your customers?
  - Does the word have another meaning that you want to avoid?
  - Is the word contextually appropriate for your customers?
  - Does the word align with your values and HR guidelines?
  - When the word is "tested," are there barriers to understanding?

- Search for "official" phonetic spelling charts to learn which words are used and which ones you'd like to adopt.
- Revisit the word list throughout the year to make sure the words remain appropriate for your customers.
- Keep in mind, a word can be "assigned" a new meaning over time and might need to be reconsidered for use with phonetic spelling.

Here's a quick self-check for you to do when reviewing a recent customer interaction.

The 5 C's of Customer Communication	
Courteous	Information was delivered with a friendly and empathetic tone, including courtesy phrases
Clear	Information was easy to follow, easy to understand, and did not lead to confusion
Concise	Information was brief, to the point, and answered the customer's question
Complete	Message included all key points to inform and update the customer
Caring	Message showed respect for the customer and was delivered with consideration for the customer as an individual, not as a "ticket"

Commanding phrases to avoid	Suggested replacements
You should look at both options and then decide. You ought to look at both options and then decide.	One suggestion is to review both options and then decide which is best for you.
You have to submit the form. You must submit the form.	The form is required when we submit your application. The reviewers are unable to process the application without the form. The form is required because it has all of the information about your recent account activity.
You have to call the pharmacy. You need to call the pharmacy.	Now that you have the code, the next step is to call the pharmacy... Now that you have the code, please call the pharmacy...
You need to talk a little louder, I can't hear you.	I was unable to hear the last four digits of your telephone number. Would you please repeat them for me?

Other phrases to avoid when communicating with customers	Suggested replacements
Bullet list	Talking points List of topics
Bullet-proof	Air-tight Cut and dried Time-tested
Dang, darn, shoot	[no replacement]
Hit the Enter key	Press Enter, then click on the first tab
Let's shoot that idea down. They killed that idea.	We chose not to use that idea.
Shooting the Customer Service video	Filming the Customer Service video
Take a stab at it	Give it a try Get started on it
To be honest with you	[no replacement] (If you're always honest with customers, there's no need to announce it.)
Words now associated with politics or politicians	[monitor regularly]

Note that these three tables offer examples for your consideration. Your organization might prefer to use different verbiage.

FROM MY NOTEBOOK

IS THERE EVER AN EXCUSE FOR TREATING CUSTOMERS POORLY?

During my two decades of reviewing thousands of calls and having follow-up conversations with CSPs, they've shared a number of reasons why a customer service experience did not meet expectations.

Summed up, the reasons would fall into one of these categories:

- The customer was rude to me.
- I was having a tough day.
- The customer wouldn't let me get my point across.
- You can't please some people, no matter how hard you try.
- I don't know what happened, the call just went off the rails.

Here's a version of the passionate plea that I deliver to CSPs:

We're here to support you as you deliver great customer service. Perfection is not required.

I can appreciate the job-related stress, extra effort needed (which is especially true during exceptional times such as the pandemic), and the skill required to stay on point with all the processes, procedures, and protocol. I get it.

But there's a line that we don't cross and that is treating our customers poorly.

The only reason I can think of that would be a true "excuse" is if you're having a breakdown during a call. The responsibility falls to leaders to help you get the help you need, do the "clean up" with the customer, learn from this incident, and put measures in place to make sure this doesn't happen again.

In all of my contact center experience, I have not had one incident that would qualify for this exception. Hearing what the exception is definitely gets the attention of CSPs though. They then realize that their "excuses" are *within their control.*

Sometimes it is challenging to maintain professional decorum in the CSP role, and there might be close calls. Having protocols in place to manage these situations and support the CSPs in order to prevent such occurrences is critical for top-quality customer service.

3. When the Answer is "No"

It's rare in Customer Service for the answer to be: No. Period.

Our job is to suggest solutions, offer options, invite interaction. So even if the answer really is "no," we use our communication skills to provide context, explain processes and procedures, confirm our concern, and suggest next steps. In other words, we find a way to say "yes" even if due to reasons beyond all control, the answer is "no."

When the answer is "no," we still want to preserve the relationship with the customer and invite them to contact us again. While the answer could be "no" to the specific ask, the answer is "yes" as to whether we appreciate the person as a customer.

Consider the following examples:

1. The outcome was not as the customer had hoped:

    - *I have the update for you, and it's not the news we were hoping for. The application was not approved. The reason given was the income listed on page 2. Again, we were hoping for a different outcome.*

- *I can appreciate how you feel about this situation. We were also hoping for a different outcome.*
- *I do have a suggestion for you. Are you interested in knowing about two organizations that may be helpful to contact for additional assistance?*

2. The organization doesn't offer what the customer is asking for:

    - *We offer [a, b, c] services (or products), but we do not offer the [x, y, z] services that you mentioned. Would you like to hear about our [a, b, c] services at this time?*

3. The organization offers the [x, y, z] services or products the customer is asking for, but they're currently unavailable:

    - *We offer [a, b, c] services, but the [x, y, z] services that you mentioned are unavailable. We expect to know by the end of the month when they will become available again. Would you like to hear about our [a, b, c] services in the meantime?*

4. The CSP has shared all of the current available options with the customer:

    - *Those are the two options that we are able to recommend. You asked if we have other suggestions...those are the only two I'm able to recommend at this time.*

Note that the above are examples for your consideration. Your organization might prefer to use different verbiage.

"No's" to avoid

- No at the beginning of the sentence.
- No because I'm the one in charge.
- No because I don't like the way you asked.
- No because I'm having a tough day.
- No because I looked and I gave up looking.
- No because I don't know where to look.

TRAINING TALK

LET'S TALK ABOUT THE "NO'S"

- Have you identified the situations where the response is "no?"
- What has been the customer feedback to hearing "no?"
- Are there barriers that can be removed for customers?
- What other options are available to customers?
- How are CSPs trained to respond when saying no?

4. Managing Challenging Situations

There's no way to sugar-coat this. We all experience challenging customer service situations. I'm talking about situations like the ones listed here. How many have you experienced?

- Dissatisfaction
- Misinformation
- Anger
- Argumentativeness
- Resistance
- Off-topic discussions
- Personal or mental health challenges
- Expressions of biases regarding the CSP
- Expressions of industry bias or disapproval
- Intended disruption, competitive snooping, revenge-seeking

I've heard story after story about challenging customer service situations. My response might surprise you (as is true for my clients):

I want to hear all about the situation, every detail. This is a great opportunity for us. I wish I could have managed the call for them.

You should see the look on their faces. Who gets energized hearing about challenging situations? I do.

Here's why:

- These situations offer CSPs the opportunity to stretch their customer service skills.
- Customer service research tells us that if we manage these situations properly, customers become even more loyal and committed (as we saw earlier with the discussion about the "service recovery paradox").
- These situations allow us to discover gaps in our training and service delivery.
- Often the one customer who speaks up is speaking on behalf of other customers who share the same feedback but don't speak up.
- If we learn from the situation, we will be better prepared for future challenges.

Mental distancing

A study published in the Journal of Experimental Social Psychology *reveals that mentally distancing yourself from the task at hand can enhance your creative insight.*
PREVENTION MAGAZINE
(Winter 2012)

When a CSP has managed a challenging situation or is required to express empathy toward a customer with an especially sad story, it helps to have a few moments of "mental distancing" before the next customer interaction.

FROM MY NOTEBOOK

AVOID LABELING THE CUSTOMER

I encourage clients to be intentional about not labeling a customer as a:

- Difficult Customer
- Disgruntled Customer
- Disruptive Customer
- Rude Customer
- Foul-mouthed Customer

Using lessons learned from our HR colleagues, we focus on the behavior or the situation and avoid labeling the customer. We're experiencing a:

✓ Challenging situation
✓ Challenging conversation
✓ Challenging interaction
✓ Customer expressing dissatisfaction
✓ Customer using inappropriate language

Let's get grounded before exploring how to manage these challenges:

- Each customer deserves the absolute best customer service we can provide.
- CSPs are trained to deliver customer service. Customers are not trained to be customers.
- Even in those situations where we must disconnect or disengage, we can remain courteous.

We've already covered the apology in the chapter on the Connection Phase. Now, let's look at changing the direction of the call or interaction during the Conversation Phase.

The interaction is stuck or goes in reverse when we hear comments like these:

- *I'm upset...*
- *Why in the world...?*
- *What are you people thinking?*
- *That makes no sense...*
- *You just don't understand...*

The CSP's task is to get the conversation into neutral.

The CSP can use phrases like these:

- *Again, we do apologize.*
- *That is understandable.*
- *It is understandable that you feel that way.*
- *I will do my best to make this right for you.*
- *I'm glad you contacted us so I can work on this for you.*

Next, move the conversation forward.

The CSP says:

- *Now, let's make sure I have all of the information.*
- *Earlier you mentioned [x, y, z]. Please tell me more about that.*
- *Is there anything else you'd like to share about the situation?*
- *To summarize, first about a..., then b..., and c...*
- *Thank you. Now let's look at some options for you.*
- *What else may I provide for you about options [1, 2, 3]?*

Last stop: Customer Satisfaction.

The CSP says:

- *You had a question about [a, b, c]. We looked at two options for you. You agreed to Option 2.*

- *Before we end the call, I want to make sure I have provided all of the information you need.*
- *I appreciate...*
- *Again, my name is [first name]. It has been my pleasure to assist you. Thank you for calling The Very Best Company.*

Disparaging Remarks

One of the goals when managing challenges is to avoid making disparaging remarks about other CSPs, the organization, and business partners. This practice reveals to customers more inside information than they need. Plus, sharing this kind of information can lead to an overall lack of confidence in your organization.

Phrases to *avoid* are:

- *Who did you speak with? I have no idea why they told you that.*
- *That team has had a lot of turnover lately, so that explains it.*
- *Well, I'm not surprised. I used to work over there and...*

TRAINING TALK

WELCOMING FEEDBACK FROM CSPs

While CSPs are asked not to share disparaging comments with customers, they are encouraged to share feedback with their leaders about customer service issues—and examples of excellent customer service.

This feedback allows your organization to:

- Track trends and address them.
- Identify gaps in service.
- Identify training topics.

- Follow up with selected customers.
- Follow up with selected CSPs and leaders.
- Follow up with related business partners and stakeholders.
- Recognize CSPs who excel at managing challenges.

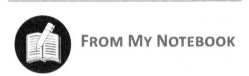

FROM MY NOTEBOOK

WHEN YOU ARE REQUIRED TO DISCONNECT OR DISENGAGE

Though I don't like to admit this, I am aware there are times when the CSP is required to disconnect or disengage from a customer. Even so, the 3-F's still apply and can be used to disengage with courtesy.

We keep these principles in mind:

- We don't label customers—we focus on the behavior or situation.
- We extend courtesy to customers. Period.
- We have no control over how the courtesy will be received.

Here's recommended verbiage:

First alert:

- *I'm happy to continue this conversation with you, but we are not allowed to participate in conversations where abusive or inappropriate language is being used.*
- *I'm happy to continue this chat with you, but we are not allowed to participate in chat conversations where abusive or inappropriate language is being used.*

Final alert:

- *I am now required to disconnect due to what my company considers abusive or inappropriate language / behavior. Goodbye. This is delivered in a neutral tone, yet with confidence.*

- *I am now required to discontinue this communication due to what my company considers abusive or inappropriate language / behavior. Goodbye.*

The key point here is the importance of having proper procedures in place to ensure the customer is "heard" and shown respect—even during challenging interactions. Be sure to include this important topic during CSP training sessions to help CSPs manage challenging situations that have potential HR or legal ramifications.

---

5. Building Relationships

In the Gladly survey discussed earlier, we noted that 69% of customers surveyed said they feel like "tickets or cases." We miss so many opportunities when we don't connect with customers and build relationships. Business benefits of building those relationships include that customers:

- ✓ Feel appreciated.
- ✓ Feel good about the decision to do business with you.
- ✓ Tell others about you.
- ✓ Want to do business with you again.
- ✓ Notice the difference between your service and the service they receive elsewhere.

How do you build business relationships when communicating with your customers?

- Use their names 1–2 times during the conversation. Their name is the best courtesy word you can use and a sure way to make a connection when used at the right times.
- Pay attention to the details that customers mention and mention them as appropriate. I called a customer service center *while traveling to Louisville, Kentucky*, and this detail

came up during my conversation with the CSP. Near the end of the call, the CSP said she hoped I had a great trip *to Louisville*. She paid attention. She treated me like a person, not a ticket. And I have a favorable view of the company based on her overall customer service delivery, especially her listening skills.

- Maintain professional boundaries when building relationships. In the example above, it was quite appropriate for the CSP to say have a great trip to Louisville. An example of an out-of-bounds comment would be: "What is taking you to Louisville?" This was my first interaction with her and our business relationship was not developed to the point of her inquiring beyond what I shared.

- From the CSPs I coach, I've learned that sometimes it works best to hold the pleasantries until the end of the call. Saving the pleasantries until the end allows the CSP to include the pleasantries with the closing as a "surprise" and to demonstrate that we care about the customer as a person, not just as a customer service issue to be resolved. Here's one of the best examples:

  While speaking with a customer, a CSP noted that the customer's birthday had been the previous day. The CSP waited until the closing and then added a friendly "Happy belated birthday." The customer was both delighted and surprised. Since the conversation focused on a matter related to the customer's medication, it was best to address the medication issues first and save the "pleasantries" for the closing.

- Remember, building relationships does not require humor, levity, or cheerleading. I'm thinking about some of the challenging situations that CSPs encounter. In an effort to "lighten the situation," CSPs might use humor, for example.

Again, think of the CSP who wished me a great trip to Louisville. She did not use humor. She used her listening skills, a friendly tone, and call management to create a connection and build a business relationship. If she had used humor, it might have come across as sarcasm.

6. Developing Skills

One day I had a meeting at a client's office building, and it was interesting that I saw not one but two former CSPs in passing. Both of them shared the same story—they used the information learned while working at the contact center to help advance their careers. Both remembered the communication skills we discussed when they were CSPs—and explained how those skills still serve them well in their new roles.

This story has been repeated by other former CSPs as well. I'm proud to say CSPs that I have trained have been selected for roles with increased responsibility, have moved on to new companies, and have advanced in their careers in ways that they could not have imagined. Here's my take on their CSP experience, their leadership, and career advancement:

1. When they were CSPs, they could see the bigger picture. When you learn how to successfully manage a challenging situation with a customer, you can use that skill with new customers, colleagues, and business partners.

2. When they were in the contact center, they sought opportunities to contribute at a higher level. They took on projects to help resolve customer service challenges. They contributed during the team meetings so their team members could learn from them.

3. They not only participated in coaching and feedback sessions,

they also sought out feedback about their performance, putting them into a continuous feedback loop.

4. They used their advanced communication skills when networking, interviewing, and presenting. With communication being one of the top skills for success, this was a sure path to building their brand and making a favorable impression.

5. They maintained their customer focus, even though the customer may have changed. One former CSP explained that her new "customer" is her internal team, and she uses lessons from our customer service conversations as she communicates with them in her leadership role.

Having learned these lessons from my former clients, I enjoy reminding current CSPs of the importance of developing their customer service skills—for the role they are in now and for career advancement. The contact center is the heart of the company and one of the best places to develop customer service, communication, and leadership skills—all of which are top skills needed when moving to roles with additional responsibility.

The Conversation Phase requires high levels of customer service skills, business acumen, Emotional Intelligence, and self-management. During this phase, the CSP seeks solutions, offers information, manages challenging situations, and builds relationships with the customer. These skills contribute to the overall customer experience, to the organizational goals, and to the CSP's professional development. The next phase is the Closure Phase, but it is much more than just a wrap up and goodbye.

CHAPTER 4

THE CLOSURE PHASE

After successfully making the connection and managing the conversation, the next phase is closure. Because the closure is at the end and may not be viewed as an "important" part of the interaction, we may miss some customer service opportunities.

During my sessions with CSPs, I have learned what they are often thinking at the close of a call or customer interaction. Here is a representative list:

- *The closing is too long, I hope they don't hang up.*
- *Oh yeah, I need to mention the survey.*
- *I need to document the customer contact.*
- *What about that follow-up item?*
- *I know I'm going to be dinged on that call during the call review.*
- *How are my customer service stats?*
- *I need a break.*
- *Gottagetreadyforthenextcustomer* [indicating how rushed they may feel].

Using the 3-F Formula, I draw my clients' attention to maximizing the closing. This is one of the most effective ways to boost customer satisfaction. Here are some closing suggestions:

How to maximize the closing	Verbiage examples
Recap	I have updated your address, shown you how to find the resource section on the new website, and provided you with updated shipment information...
Friendly reminders	As a reminder, we will call you Thursday afternoon to confirm...
Additional assistance	Is there anything else I may do to assist you?
Additional information	Do you have any additional questions about our new website?
Check-in	I want to make sure that we've covered everything on your list today...
Acknowledge earlier apology with update	Thank you again for bringing the shipment issue to our attention and for accepting our apology. I have made the correction and as you requested, I will call you on Monday.
Full-circle communication	Earlier you mentioned that you wanted to share some feedback about the email we sent you. Would you like to share your feedback at this time?
Appreciation	It has been a pleasure to assist you with your question about the website and thank you for the feedback about the email.

How to maximize the closing	Verbiage examples
Branding	Thank you for calling The Very Best Company. Thank you for contacting The Very Best Company.
Making a positive lasting impression	[Result: The customer's reaction after the closing, recalling this was a memorable experience where they were treated like a person and not a ticket, where your organization is set apart from all the others.]

Note that these are examples for your consideration. Your organization might prefer to use different verbiage.

The closing is more than "goodbye." It is more than a check-off on the call flow. The closing is important for reminding customers about your great customer service delivery, showing appreciation, and leaving them with a positive lasting impression.

Should you use a more personal close?

- *Have a nice day.*
- *Have a great day.*
- *Have a nice evening.*
- *Have a nice weekend.*
- *Have a good holiday.*

The list of personal closes has expanded over the years. It started with "Have a nice day" and now the list includes references to people's weekends, holidays, vacations, and beyond. I'm expecting any time now to hear a movie fan say, "Have a wonderful life."

You guessed it. I'm not a fan of the personal close. When I gently suggest that the personal close may not be the best option to use during some business calls and written communication, CSPs respond with passion. They have emphatically said they don't want to give up the personal close, not even for their favorite Customer Service Consultant.

Keeping the customer in mind, I have developed a list of requirements for the use of the personal close:

- Is it appropriate for that customer?
- Is it appropriate as a follow-on to the service provided?
- Is it placed *before* the business close?

Instead of this (putting the personal close last):

- *Thank you for calling The Very Best Company.*
- *Have a nice day.*

Say this, assuming the three requirements above are met (putting the business close last):

- *Have a nice day and thank you for calling The Very Best Company.*

Here are some updated options, using an expanded business close:

- I've enjoyed speaking with you today. Thank you for calling The Very Best Company.
- We appreciate your business. Thank you for calling The Very Best Company.
- It's been a pleasure to speak with you today. Thank you for calling The Very Best Company.

Notice how these examples touch on all three F's. They have a *friendly* tone, use *formal* language, and are *focused* specifically on the interaction with the customer.

FROM MY NOTEBOOK

THE CHALLENGE WITH THE PERSONAL CLOSE

I'm reminded of the time I purchased a money order made payable to a funeral home. During the informal conversation with the teller, two things were clear: We had a death in the family, and I was headed to Alabama that weekend. The money order was processed, checked, and okayed. What happened next?

The teller closed with: *"Have a nice weekend!"*

This is a good example of exactly what CSPs want to avoid when using a personal close. While this may have been the teller's "standard" closing statement, it was not the best choice for that interaction. The teller's tone sounded like I had requested the money order before leaving for a vacation, not a funeral.

I remind CSPs of this lesson when they communicate with a customer in a difficult or unfortunate situation, such as when their medication was not delivered on time and the customer is panicking. Or when saying "no" to a customer. In these and similar situations, a personal closing such as "Have a great weekend!" will likely sound like a flippant remark and will make for a poor customer experience.

THE CLUTTERED VS. UNCLUTTERED CLOSING

The Cluttered Version

A cluttered closing is one where the verbal exchanges get "stuck" in a loop, the branding is diluted, and there appears to be little additional benefit for the customer. Here's an example, presented for demonstration purposes only:

CSP: *Have a nice day and thank you for calling The Very Best Company.*

Customer: *You too, you have a nice day. It's been great to talk to you.*

CSP: *Thank you. It's been great to talk to you too.*

Customer: *I was so impressed with you. This was much better than talking to other companies.*

CSP: *How nice of you to say that. We enjoy hearing that kind of feedback.*

Customer: *You should. You all are the best.*

CSP: *You're the best too. Thank you very much.*

Customer: *You're welcome.*

CSP: *Well, thank you again.*

Customer: *You too. Bye-bye.*

CSP: *You're welcome. Bye.*

The Uncluttered Version

Here's an "after" version with edits. When you compare the before and after, you will notice that the "edits" are made in the CSP verbiage only. There is no expectation for the customer to know how to manage the closing—that's the CSP's job. You will also notice that the words in bold—the use of the customer's name and the statement about sharing comments with the team—both make a big difference.

CSP: *It's been my pleasure to assist you today* **[customer's name]**. *Thank you for calling The Very Best Company.*

Customer: *Have a nice day. It's been great to talk to you.*

CSP: *Thank you. It's been great to talk to you too.*

Customer: *I was so impressed with you. This was much better than talking to other companies.*

CSP: *Thank you! We enjoy hearing feedback from our customers. **I will share this with the team.** And once again, thank you for calling The Very Best Company [to be said with the most pleasant tone].*

Customer: *Bye-bye.*

CSP: *Goodbye.*

In this example it helps to use the customer's name, mirror the customer's response, and state that you will share the feedback with the team. Repeating the business close is an eloquent way to break out of the loop. In addition to the word choice, tone is important here. Avoid sounding rushed or dismissive at all costs.

> **IT IS IMPORTANT TO CONTINUE TO MANAGE THE CALL WITH SKILL, EVEN DURING THE CLOSING.**

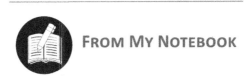

FROM MY NOTEBOOK

GOODBYE

As a Customer Service Consultant, one of the first changes I request of clients is to discontinue using "Bye-bye." Especially the "Bye-bye" that sounds like the childhood version.

"Bye-bye" is definitely informal, and it can dilute your business close.

The winning replacement (even though it may "feel" a bit stuffy) is a simple "Goodbye."

Another option for a less formal approach is "Bye."

Also an option:

> **CSP:** *It has been my pleasure to speak with you today. Thank you for calling The Very Best Company.*
>
> **Customer:** *Thank you too, bye-bye now.*
>
>> [You can tell the Customer considers the conversation finished and is disconnecting.]
>
> **CSP:** *[no response required in some cases]*

Clients who have tested this approach have been pleasantly surprised at how "clean" this closing is. They typically are relieved, knowing they're not going to get into a "communication loop." This works best when the CSP has already stated the business close and it's clear the customer is pleased with the experience and is disconnecting.

TRAINING TALK

CLUTTERED CLOSINGS

During a recent training program for CSPs, one of our activities was to present a "performance" of a cluttered closing. We exaggerated a bit for "entertainment purposes," and it was entertaining indeed.

During the performances, I was the CSP and the participants served as the customers. I could hardly get through the activity without laughing. The participants playing the role as the customer were thanking me profusely and then sharing multiple personal closings and advice, encouraging me to take care of myself during the pandemic (even reminding me of the guidelines from the public health professionals). The advice was enough to last for quite some time.

The CSPs could definitely relate to that loop. After the stellar performances, I shared how to get out of the loop, gracefully. I highly recommend this activity for training—and for some moments of levity.

TRAINING TALK

THE MATCHING GAME

When customers share compliments, I encourage CSPs to match their verbiage. This shows the use of listening skills, that the responses are aligned to the compliments, and that responses aren't canned or scripted but are customer-focused. This is a tried and true technique.

It's also a great training activity. It's fun to play the Matching Game using real-life examples from recent customer interactions.

Customer: *Thank you very much.*

CSP: *You're very welcome [name]. It was my pleasure.*

Customer: *You are the best Customer Service person I've ever spoken to...*

CSP: *Thank you for your kind words [name]. It has been a pleasure to speak with you as well.*

Customer: *You are the best. Tell your supervisor you deserve a raise!*

CSP: *Thank you for the compliment [name]. It's great to know you're pleased with our Customer Service. I will share your suggestion with my supervisor.*

Customer: *I don't know what I would do without you. You really took care of everything I needed today.*

CSP: *That's what we're here for, to be of service to you [name]. It was my pleasure to take care of everything you needed today.*

FROM MY NOTEBOOK

KIND WORDS FROM CUSTOMERS

Here are some kind words from customers about My Awesome Clients:

- She was the most professional CSP ever. You all are fortunate to have her on your team.
- The way the CSP responded helped to ease my mind about my personal situation.
- A Healthcare Professional (HCP) said she was very pleased with the CSP. She was professional and provided all of the information the HCP needed.
- The CSP went the extra mile.
- The CSP reaffirmed my confidence in your company.
- To the CSP: You deserve a raise.

Note: I've edited the comments in light of my commitment to confidentiality. Plus, I'm using the title of Customer Service Professional in all of the examples.

From a customer, who was almost without words
when expressing appreciation to Davina,
a Customer Service Professional in California:
"I want to give you an electronic hug."

The Closure Phase is more than just saying goodbye and moving on to the next customer, the next task. There are opportunities within those few minutes to brand the calls and make a lasting impression. Within each closing you can embed an invitation for the customer to return to do business with you again.

You have now completed Part One of the *Customer Communication*

Formula, where you focused on the 3-F Formula and how to apply the 3-F's to the three phases: Connection. Conversation. Closure. You have gained insights from the special feature sections *From My Notebook* and *Training Talk.*

This is a good time to pause to reflect on what you and your organization are already doing to create positive customer experiences.

This is also a good time to pause and reflect on how you will begin to apply the 3-F Formula.

- What will you do differently during your next customer interaction, based on what you learned about the 3-F Formula and the three phases?
- What is your plan for applying the formula to all of your customer interactions going forward?
- How will you apply the formula across all channels?

In Part Two, Customer Service leaders and CSPs are invited to participate in the Customer Service Consultation. Now that you know how to use the 3-F Formula to create great customer experiences, a next step is to look at your customer service program from a more strategic level. This means that you will use the formula to guide individual customer interactions *and* to influence your overall approach to customer relations.

PART TWO

THE CUSTOMER SERVICE CONSULTATION

CHAPTER 5

12 QUESTIONS FOR REFLECTION

Congratulations on choosing to make next-level customer service a top priority. This consultation will help you discover the strengths as well as the gaps in your current process so that you can build your way forward and apply the 3-F's in the most efficient manner.

While the consultation chapters are intended for customer service leaders, CSPs will also find this information beneficial, especially if their professional development goals include moving to leadership positions. As I mentioned earlier, many of the CSPs I have worked with have indeed found themselves in new roles and leadership positions.

There are two parts to this self-guided consultation. In this chapter, we begin with 12 Questions for Reflection that guide you through an in-depth discussion about your customer service brand, leadership, and culture. In the following chapter, I introduce the 10 Customer Service Statements Every Organization Needs.

If you lead a customer service organization, I recommend that you review both consultation chapters in their entirety and "engage" in the self-guided consultation process. If your organization is in the process of merging, reorganizing, responding to recent critical feedback, or addressing CSP engagement, you will find that this review provides the framework to uncover, process, and address the situation, whatever it might be.

And even if your organization has a well-established customer service brand, consider reading this and the next chapter for any opportunities to think about your brand in a new way. As you participate in this consultation, one suggestion is to invite selected leaders, stakeholders, and Customer Service Professionals to join you as appropriate. Before you begin the consultation, let's do an assessment to gain clarity on your vision.

Looking at the recent customer feedback, reports, stakeholder input, and suggestions from CSPs, what are your top three reasons for taking your customer service to the next level?

Consider coming back to these reasons whenever you need a reminder of why you're going through this process. You're likely to experience internal and external challenges as you assess your customer service delivery, so you will appreciate reflecting on the reasons you've chosen to head down this path in the first place.

What is your channel?

Another question to ask yourself is what channels you want to focus on for the delivery of your new and improved customer service. According to Gladly (gladly.com), an organization researching customer experiences and preferences, these are the most popular channels:

- Voice
- IVR
- Self-Service
- Text
- Chat
- In-App Chat
- Social Media
- Email

Even with all the additional channels as options, in my experience, most customers still choose to pick up the phone and speak to a live CSP when contacting customer service. This was confirmed in the 2019 Gladly Customer Expectations Report.[7] This is why the phone is my focus throughout this book. Given that most customers use the phone, a top priority for your organization is to make sure your CSPs' phone skills are outstanding.

If you've added additional customer service channels and are looking for new ways to approach customer service, the 3-F Formula is a great place to start. Keep in mind, your customers expect the same great service, no matter the channel.

A recent assignment with one of my clients provides further insights. The client, who knew about my programs for phone-based customer service, asked me to revise their written customer communications. I followed the 3-F Formula. I made sure the verbiage had a friendly "tone," was formal, and focused. The client was pleased, and the new verbiage was fully approved after an internal review.

FROM MY NOTEBOOK

INTERACTIVE VOICE RESPONSE (IVR)

The customer experience begins before the customer calls or contacts your organization. It begins with the salesperson, website, social media, advertisements, word of mouth, or your company's Interactive Voice Response (IVR) system.

---

7. "The 2019 Customer Expectations Report," Gladly (https://www.gladly.com/blog/2019-customer-expectations-report/).

Of all the touchpoints prior to the customer's interaction with the CSP, one of the touchpoints you typically manage or influence is the IVR. For your consideration:

- Think of the recording as a preview of what is to come during the customer interaction and apply the 3-F Formula here as well.
- It helps to have a custom recording, not a heard-it-all-before recording with your-call-is-important-to-us verbiage, because you want to set yourself apart, even at this early touchpoint.
- Show appreciation to the customer for contacting your organization, for the willingness to stand by until they are connected, and for following the IVR instructions.
- Be careful about using acronyms and company jargon. This might create unnecessary barriers for the customer.
- Test the recording with selected CSPs and customers. Ask how to make this touchpoint friendlier.
- Be strategic about what the customer hears on hold. Company information? Music? Silence? Or a choice?
- Make sure you and your CSPs experience the on-hold process from the customer's point of view.
- Finally, revisit your recording frequently and make changes as your business needs change. This is important as you gather additional feedback from customers and business partners about their on-hold experiences.

A bottom line about your bottom line

Customer service is important to the success of your organization. Here are some key statistics from a Gladly customer survey that reinforce the value of excellent customer service as it relates to your bottom line.[8]

---

8. "The 2019 Customer Expectations Report," Gladly (https://www.gladly.com/blog/2019-customer-expectations-report/).

- 84% of customers say they will switch to another company after three poor customer service experiences.
- 77% say they would buy from a company again because of outstanding service versus a great marketing campaign.
- 74% of customers base their purchase decisions on customer service experience.
- 69% feel that they have been treated like a "ticket" instead of a real person.
- 63% report switching to a competitor because of a better customer service experience.

As the Gladly Customer Expectations Report shows[9], customer service can absolutely win or lose customers. This is an open and shut issue. When you meet or exceed your customers' expectations, your bottom line will reflect that success.

For this reason, I teach a "people first" approach to customer service. How your customers perceive your brand determines whether they will buy from you in the future, recommend your brand to their friends, and most importantly, make positive connections between your brand and what you sell. Now let's look at the 12 Questions.

THE 12 QUESTIONS

Keep in mind that your answers to the following questions will set the tone for achieving the outcome you want. You're encouraged to be transparent and detailed when answering the questions.

1. **We know the first rule of customer service is that the customer comes first. So let's start there. Who is your primary customer?**

---

9. "The 2019 Customer Expectations Report," Gladly (https://www.gladly.com/blog/2019-customer-expectations-report/).

Customer is the term used for the person with whom you are doing business.

If your organization sells products, typically the person you do business with is considered a customer.

If your organization offers services, typically the customer is considered a client.

In some industries, customers are given specialized names. For example, in healthcare, you serve patients. In higher education, students are typically considered your primary customers.

The following table provides a list of some specialized names for your reference.

Organization or industry	Customer or client
Bank	Banker/client
Church, faith community	Member
Consulting/legal/financial services	Client
Consumer goods	Consumer
Credit union	Member
Education	Student
Elected officials	Constituent
Healthcare	Patient
Hotel/hospitality	Guest
Internet/subscription service	Subscriber
Library/bookstore	Reader/guest/customer
Park	Visitor
Professional services	Client
Radio/podcast	Listener
Restaurant	Guest
Retail	Shopper/guest
Television network	Viewer
Transportation	Passenger/rider/frequent flyer
Website	Visitor
CharlottePurvis.com	My Awesome Clients—some of the best clients in the world

2. **How do you refer to the customer?**

   Are you doing so in a respectful and appreciative manner?

   Or are you just calling everyone a generic customer, without considering a more specialized category for them (using the examples listed above)?

3. **Is there an option to have a branded name for your customer or client?**

   Has your branding team suggested a branded name for the customer? Using one gives your organization an opportunity to enhance your reputation and boost your customer service brand.

   Here's an example of giving customers a branded name. Suppose your company, The Very Best Company, is a retailer. Your customers could be called The Very Best Shoppers. Then, when you post an announcement on your website with a special offer, instead of greeting them with "Dear Customer," you greet them with "Dear Very Best Shopper."

   Immediately, your customers are reminded of your brand and the underlying message they receive is that they are a part of a community of customers. This may seem subtle, but when it comes to giving customers a warm feeling of belonging, subtle differences can give you the edge.

   One lesson about job titles and brand names is to select titles and names that have meaning for the customer, not those that are just related to your operations. As an example, a job title with the word "case" in it (Case Analyst) would not be recommended. That title might reflect your internal processes, but customers don't want to feel like they are a "case" that is being managed.

Popular sock company Bombas offers an example of positive brand naming. Bombas (the name comes from the Latin word for "bumblebees") refers to their customers as members of The Hive. Their customer service team is called the Bombas Customer Happiness Team.

Being part of The Hive is not just a marketing gimmick. Bombas makes customers feel connected to their brand, not just to the socks and apparel they purchase. The company does "good" as well. For every pair of socks purchased, a pair is donated to someone affected by homelessness.

As a member of The Hive and a Bombas Customer Service Enthusiast, I can report that the company is an outstanding example of connecting with the customer and the community. While I was writing this book, I had several interactions with the Bombas Customer Happiness Team and appreciated observing their approach to delighting customers.

4. **What is most important to your customers?**

When rating your customer service, how do your customers rank these and other criteria?

- *Friendliness*
- *Courtesy*
- *Ease of use*
- *Channels offered*
- *Length of time to resolution*

Now, think of your customers as *people*. What is on their minds this week? What challenges are they facing in their lives? When they contact you, they are doing so as people first, then as customers. It helps to keep this in mind when communicating with them.

5. **How do you use the information about the things that are important to your customers? How is your team meeting these expectations?**

    How often do leaders have deep-dive conversations about what is important to customers? Do you include customer perspectives in your next-level presentations? Are you recognizing outstanding CSPs based on their attention to customer expectations and customer priorities? During your team meetings, do you acknowledge CSPs for communicating with customers as people first?

 **FROM MY NOTEBOOK**

NATIONAL CUSTOMER SERVICE WEEK

Here's a question I ask at some point during nearly all of my consulting engagements: How do you celebrate Customer Service Week (the first full week in October)?

Using the 12 Questions and the 10 Customer Service Statements as a foundation, how about hosting a Customer Service Summit in advance of Customer Service Week each year? The summit could conclude with a Customer Service Celebration—celebrating your customers and CSPs.

For more information about Customer Service Week, visit: https://wp.csweek.com/.

---

6. **Now, let's turn to the organization. What is the Customer Service mission? Vision?**

   Do you include guiding statements about mission, vision, and values in your presentations, your reports, your critical conversations? If I visited your office or your CSPs in their remote working environments, would I see these guiding statements posted?

   Here is a key question for you and the leadership team: Do you live out your values every day?

FROM MY NOTEBOOK

LIVING OUT YOUR VALUES

As you can imagine, I have seen multiple approaches to organizational values. The following are common ones:

1. The values are rarely mentioned and were clearly written years ago as a checklist item
2. The values are mentioned but only when there's a conflict
3. The values are listed but not lived
4. The values are listed and lived
5. The values are listed, lived, and looked upon for inspiration

For your consideration, here's a checklist:

- ☐ Do you value your values?
- ☐ Do you live out your values every day?
- ☐ Do your values spotlight your customers?
- ☐ Do you display your values throughout the organization?

7. **How would you describe an ideal customer experience for your customer, one that is offered to each customer across all channels?**

   Be specific when you describe the experience. What will the experience sound like? What will it feel like? What is the outcome you're looking to achieve?

FROM MY NOTEBOOK

WHAT DO YOU CALL YOUR CUSTOMER SERVICE?

In addition to Customer Service, organizations use terms like Customer Experience, Customer Happiness, and Customer Care. One of my favorite terms is Customer Success. Whatever you decide, use my 3-F Formula to help develop the mindset for Customer Service Professionals so they know how to create great experiences for customers, no matter what term is used.

---

8. **What's driving the need for excellent customer service?**

   Remember my client who didn't want their CSPs to sound like they were at home chatting with family and friends? Another client was obsessed with the fact that a competitor had better CSATs (Customer Satisfaction scores) and wanted to focus on improving their own CSATs. Still another client left one company with a high-quality customer service brand to work for another company and wanted to make sure the new company also had a reputable brand.

What are the concerns from your stakeholders? It would help to identify their perceptions about customer service, gather additional details, and get the right internal and external people in place to relieve any "perceived pain" related to customer service delivery.

As the social media acronym SWYD suggests—Stop What You're Doing and get on this right away. What do you want to *stop doing* right away? What do you want to *start doing* right away? Finding answers to these questions is one of the most important outcomes of this consultation.

9. **When you communicate with CSPs in team meetings, huddles, one-to-one, or via email, what is the underlying theme of your messages?**

I like to think in terms of 5 P's:

- *People—CSPs, customers, stakeholders*
- *Product or service*
- *Process*
- *Profitability*
- *Perceived pettiness (topics that CSPs might consider unimportant)*

As you plan your next communication, consider the 5 P's. If you lead with people—the first P—you're setting yourself up for a win. Seek their input about what is important and what they need to hear from you in your written and verbal communication—and how often they need to hear it.

Remember, the CSPs are internal customers and are integral to your success. It is important for them to know that you care about who they are and the role they play and that you are all in this together, sharing ownership of your success.

10. What is your Customer Service story?

Even if your organization has a well-known or compelling origin story, you also want to be able to tell a story specific to customer service. Think about where customer service fits into the secret sauce of the organization.

Here are key questions to consider:

- *When did your organization start delivering customer service?*
- *What was the mission and vision then?*
- *How has your focus changed over the years?*
- *What was the defining moment for your organization?*
- *What was that one customer conversation that taught you a customer service lesson that you still use today?*

You can share this story on your organization's website, tell the story to new team members, and include portions of your story in presentations. Telling your story will give listeners another perspective on *why you do what you do*. Plus, it becomes the thread that joins all of you together—current, former, and future team members.

AS AN AUTHOR AND CONSULTANT, I SHARE MY STORY WITH YOU IN THE FINAL CHAPTER OF THIS BOOK, "THE FORMULA AND ME."

Now let's turn to you:

- *What is your personal customer service story?*
- *What path did you take to arrive in your role?*
- *When you are the customer, what is the experience like?*
- *Do you have any customer service memories from childhood?*
- *Did you work in the service industry early on in your career?*
- *Did you ever have your own business?*
- *What do you enjoy most about customer service?*
- *What is unique about what you bring to the team?*

FROM MY NOTEBOOK

YOUR CUSTOMER SERVICE STORY

Knowing how important customer service is to your organization's branding and bottom line, consider using your influence to educate all employees about your contact center. One idea is to develop a contact center presentation to be included in the onboarding training across the organization. Be sure to include your story and recent customer testimonials the company has received.

Did you win an award for your excellent customer service? Were you featured in a recent publication? Have you developed a training innovation that can be adapted by other teams? I hope you'll share these and other points of pride in your presentation.

To add even more range and depth, consider recording a model call or developing an example from another channel, bringing your customer service brand to life. For privacy concerns, this is highly recommended over using an actual customer interaction—even if masked.

11. Have you personally experienced your customer service delivery firsthand?

If you have ever seen the popular television show *Undercover Boss*, you understand the benefits of experiencing your customer service process firsthand. When you go through the process yourself, the strengths and gaps in your CSP training program will become immediately obvious. On the show, the bosses go to extraordinary lengths to disguise their appearances. This may not be an option for you. You can also get some great intel using approved mystery shoppers or family members as appropriate to find out what the typical customer service experience is like.

Here are some additional questions to ask:

- *Do you and other leaders conduct call simulations a few times a year? This is especially important when you launch a new product or service.*
- *Have you listened to your Interactive Voice Response (IVR) message recently?*
- *Have you read the customer service information included on your organization's website? On social media?*

By now, I hope you know where I'm going with this. As a Customer Service leader, have you put yourself in your customers' shoes? If not, make it a priority to learn about your customer service firsthand or at least secondhand. You owe this to your customers. And as a leader, you owe this to yourself.

12. Does everyone on the team understand the connection between Customer Service and their livelihood? (Time for some straight talk.)

This last question may surprise you, but it is the moment in our consultation that brings it all home. Sometimes what we all need is some plain talk and a leader who knows how to "keep it real." The point here is that we don't want CSPs to act as though they're doing the customer a favor by delivering great customer service. If this is the attitude, then whenever a customer voices a complaint, disappointment, or frustration— oh my—it is as though the sky is falling.

In the worst-case scenarios, the customer is in the middle of an "us vs. them" conversation where the "us" team must win. When I review calls with this dynamic, I wonder if everyone understands this about the "us vs. them" connection: Without "them," there can be no "us."

Here's a principle that I share, and I'm pleased to say that I've only had to do so a few times in my career:

IT IS VERY LIKELY THAT YOU NEED THEM
MORE THAN THEY NEED YOU.

Again, does everyone on your team understand that it is a privilege to be of service to the customer, to represent your organization, to grow and develop professionally? Do they make the connection between their customer service and their livelihood? The answer is embedded in the way they communicate with the customer. If I were to have the privilege of reviewing your customer communication, I would be able to answer these questions very quickly.

I would listen for the following critical incidents or anything similar that leads to customer dissatisfaction:

- *The customer hung up or disengaged abruptly after feeling judged or ignored*
- *The customer expresses disappointment with your organization*
- *The customer was treated like a "ticket" or a "case"*
- *Customer service procedures were not followed*
- *Misinformation was shared*
- *The CSP displayed rudeness, indifference, or disrespect*
- *The CSP appeared to be experiencing a personal challenge and "took it out" on the customer*
- *The CSP used inappropriate language*
- *A communication breakdown occurred, and the CSP was unable to manage through*
- *The customer mentions no longer wanting to do business with your organization*

If any of these incidents were observed, I would suggest that you shift your focus to manage the potential customer service crisis. Where are the "first responders" in your organization who can train, coach, and influence the CSPs so that they avoid these and other critical incidents at all costs?

Typically, these leaders make up the "first responder" team:

- *Managers*
- *Trainers*
- *Team Leaders*
- *QA Professionals*
- *Subject Matter Experts*
- *Internal Consultants*
- *External Consultants*
- *HR Professionals*

Whatever the configuration of your team, the key factors for turning things around are:

- **Responsiveness**: *Prepare enough people so that the response is swift*
- **Skill**: *Train the team and conduct simulations to ensure the highest level of skill*
- **Fairness**: *Manage the situation using your organizational guidelines and HR principles*
- **Influence**: *Make sure team members have strong personal brands and extensive leadership experience*
- **Calibration**: *Make sure the team is aligned on standards, expectations, and best practices*

As a leader, please emphasize that customer service is the heartbeat of your organization. It is a privilege to be of service to the customer. There are many choices out there, so remember, and I repeat, we likely need "them" more than they need "us" and without "them," there is no "us."

Bonus Question

Is the customer a regular part of your conversations?

Think back to your recent meetings with your team. Was the customer mentioned in any way? What about customer feedback? Any insight about how to be of better service to the customer? A recent customer testimonial?

Customer service teams can spend a lot of time talking about processes and procedures with no mention of the customer. This really gets my attention, and I hope it will get your attention going forward as well. As a customer-focused organization, be sure to keep the customer at the center of everything you do.

Here's a Pop Quiz

How would you most likely fill in this blank?

The customer is always _____.

Yes, the answer is "right." The customer is always right. This much-quoted statement reminds us where we should focus our attention when delivering customer service.

I always use two blanks when I present the statement though:

The customer is always _____ _____.

The answer for my two blanks is: The customer is always *the customer*.

The intent of that original quote is understandable. But the point is not whether the customer is "right." CSPs aren't always right. Leaders aren't always right. With humility I'll add, neither are consultants. But here's what we know: Our customers are our customers, and they don't receive training to be a customer.

By contrast, CSPs are trained. With the right training, they have the skills to manage customer interactions and represent the organization well. The fact is, customers are not required to be right all the time. And regardless of whether we agree with them, we are expected to make every effort to treat them with respect and create positive experiences for them.

THE CUSTOMER IS ALWAYS THE CUSTOMER.
IT IS OUR PLEASURE TO BE OF SERVICE TO THEM.

Now that you have addressed the 12 Questions and completed the first part of your self-guided consultation about your brand, your leadership, and your company culture, do you need to take a deeper dive with any of these questions? Or are you ready to learn about the 10 Customer Service Statements Every Organization Needs?

Take whatever time you need to reflect on your answers to the 12 Questions before continuing on to the 10 Statements.

CHAPTER 6

10 CUSTOMER SERVICE STATEMENTS EVERY ORGANIZATION NEEDS

As a Customer Service Consultant, I have moved around from organization to organization focusing mostly on CSPs. Now, I'm spending more time with leaders. Why? Because of another lesson I have learned:

CUSTOMER SERVICE DOESN'T BEGIN WITH THE GREETING. CUSTOMER SERVICE BEGINS WITH THE LEADERSHIP.

Leaders have a clear vision for taking the organization from where it is now to where they want to be in a year, five years, or ten years down the road. To develop your vision as a leader, a suggestion is to begin with clarity around the 10 Customer Service Statements. These ten statements help you and your team explain what you do, why you do it, and the expectations for how the customer is treated. They also set the tone for how to communicate appropriately with the customer.

THE 10 CUSTOMER SERVICE STATEMENTS

1. A mission statement about Customer Service, Customer Care, and the overall Customer Experience

    What is it that you do and why do you do it?

2. A values statement

    What do you believe in and what is most important?

3. Your expectations for customer interactions

    How will each customer be greeted and treated?

4. Your vision for Customer Service

    What do you want to be known for by your customers and what do you want to become in your industry?

5. A leadership statement

    What is the commitment of the leaders with regard to the customers and the CSPs?

6. Your Customer Service story

    What is your story, that inside look at your customer service that reflects your vision, values, viewpoints?

7. Your Customer Service tagline—shared over and over

    What is a catchy phrase that people will remember and relate to?

8. A statement of what is not acceptable for your customer service delivery

What are those 5–10 quality issues that you consider unacceptable and require your immediate attention?

9. Your Customer Service deal breakers

   What requires immediate HR attention, legal review, or further action?

10. Your approach to training and development

    What can CSPs expect for onboarding, training, coaching, mentoring, and development?

FROM MY NOTEBOOK

WAXELENE: TOP QUALITY CUSTOMER CARE

Waxelene is one of my top five all-time favorite companies, and I'm proud to be a Waxelene customer. Every aspect of their customer care is commendable—from their products to their customer service, from my interactions with the team to their company values, from how they demonstrate their customer care to how they communicate. They exemplify top quality customer care.

They relate to their customers as human beings, not just as buyers or shoppers. During the COVID-19 pandemic, for example, they sent an empathetic message reminding us how important it is to moisturize after washing our hands or using hand sanitizer. They positioned their product in the context of what was going on in the lives of their customers—in real time. They've shared other messages focusing on current events while revealing more insights about the heart of the company.

The Waxelene story is brief, and yet it tells us everything we need to know about what they do and why. The customer communication and the customer service that I have experienced align with what I have read about the Waxelene brand and mission. As a customer and Customer Service Enthusiast, it has been a privilege to be a recipient of their top-quality customer care.

───────────────────

After developing your 10 Customer Service Statements, here are ways to use them:

- Customer Service leadership in-depth discussions
- Presentations to your next-level leaders
- Huddles with CSPs
- Onboarding presentations
- Updates and reports
- Presentations to consultants and business partners
- Your personal reflections and check-ins throughout the year
- Boosting your customer service brand

Congratulations on completing the self-guided consultation. Now let's move forward to what I call "Extreme Customer Service."

CHAPTER 7

EXTREME CUSTOMER SERVICE

This chapter is dedicated to Customer Service Professionals serving on the frontlines during the COVID-19 global health crisis of 2020.

While I was writing this book, we faced a global health crisis due to COVID-19. Times like this often create a need for what I call "Extreme Customer Service," a concept that I have shared with some of my clients.

5-STEP PROCESS FOR EXTREME CUSTOMER SERVICE

*This was the May 13, 2020 email header from Gladly (**gladly.com**) This header says it all.*

⟫ Gladly	**9:15 AM**
Customer service is so important right now.	

Extreme Customer Service is a 5-step process recommended for critical situations, either external or internal. The process requires the absolute highest level of customer service that your organization can provide. Externally, it might be something on a global, national, regional, or local level, like a global health crisis or a major weather-related incident. Internally, it might be something like a quality issue. Or discontinuation or shortage of a particular product or service. Or it might be "headline news" that has resulted in bad publicity and lots of rumors being floated. On the good news side, it could be the launch of a breakthrough product or service. How should CSPs deal with the high call volume from customers wanting to know what's really going on inside your organization?

Consider using this 5-step process as a foundation when responding to critical situations.

1. Choose a select group of CSPs

First of all, you want to start with the best of the best. Put together an Extreme Customer Service team made up of CSPs who have demonstrated consistency in providing the highest level of customer service. Current high Customer Satisfaction scores are important, but you want to look for team members who have consistently delivered excellent customer service over a long period of time.

2. Develop a refresher training program

Once your organization has settled on a solution (probably after consulting with PR, HR, and your legal team) for the critical event that triggered the need for Extreme Customer Service, it's time to train your CSPs on exactly what to say and how to say it.

Strong guidance here is key. Provide your select team with scripts and verbiage to use when discussing the critical situation with customers. Make sure they know who they can look to for support during this potentially stressful time at work.

3. **Be sure to seek buy-in from your select team of CSPs**

When you offer your top CSPs this opportunity to be part of the select team, be sure that they are in agreement with taking on this task. Seek confirmation that they are on board with your solution, are ready and willing to undergo extra training, and that the timing is right from a personal perspective. For example, if one of your CSPs with high Customer Satisfaction scores over time is facing a personal or family crisis, this might not be the right time to assume an Extreme Customer Service role.

4. **Conduct extra quality reviews during this time**

Your CSPs also need consistent, quality feedback on their customer service delivery during times of crisis. Whatever your regular schedule is for reviewing customer interactions, you will want to increase it to make sure that you are getting a broad but significant snapshot of the quality of these interactions. During the initial phase, I recommend daily reviews and frequent updates for the team.

5. **Recognize and reward strong performance**

Regardless of whether your organization is in crisis mode, it's just good business practice to recognize and reward strong performance. But rewarding your CSPs is especially important during these types of extreme situations. Acknowledge that you are putting your best Customer Service Professionals on the front line to help protect the image of your company.

Also, keep in mind that the most beneficial reward may not be monetary. Your select team may first want to hear that they are doing a great job and feel sincere appreciation coming from leaders like you. It will also help to offer a reward with personal meaning for the CSP or to arrange a meaningful experience for the team. Whatever you choose, just be sure to recognize and reward your select Extreme Customer Service team throughout and upon completion of this special assignment.

After the Situation Is Resolved

As you focus on resolving the current crisis, make sure you are also thinking about the future. If you follow the Extreme Customer Service process above, you are creating a protocol and system that you can come back to as needed. This is why it's important to keep track of the steps you take now, compile the lessons learned, and properly document everything for future use.

Client Lessons Learned from Previous Experience

I have been impressed while guiding Customer Service leaders through moments of crisis or during a major event, for example. It has been a privilege to walk with my clients on this journey. It's a pleasure to share some of the lessons of Extreme Customer Service.

First, this might be a good time to bring in an external consultant who can help you navigate the situation. None of us could have predicted the way the COVID-19 pandemic would affect all of us globally. It's clear that having a broader, outside perspective to lend ideas and aid in building a successful strategy is a smart business move. When we are too close to a situation, it's easy to miss crucial points that might be "right in front of us," so consider engaging an external consultant.

Also, it is imperative to complete step 2 above. The team absolutely needs a custom training just for this Extreme Customer Service experience. Recalling successful client projects, I can highly recommend that your training includes these components:

- Leadership perspectives and expectations for the team
- Process and procedures that are relevant
- Emotional Intelligence topics (examples: self-awareness, self-regulation, empathy)
- Self-care and balance and boundaries maintenance
- Expectations for teamwork
- Customer service skills refresher
- Simulations and feedback sessions

So what can you expect when you put together your team and offer this Extreme Customer Service experience?

If you expect 100% perfection on each and every customer contact, you're likely to be disappointed. While it is Extreme Customer Service, it won't be "Perfect Customer Service." What will be different, however, is that you will conduct more reviews and more follow-ups with those customers who are not satisfied with the service they received. And you will perform more follow-ups with CSPs plus have more micro training sessions and huddles. It will be a continuous improvement loop.

The second thing that you can expect is the need for more support. Remember, the people you are putting on the frontline during this critical period in your company will need and deserve more support. So my suggestion here is just as you have CSPs who have been chosen for this opportunity, make sure that you have Customer Service leaders who have gone through the proper leadership training and preparation to provide instant support every single hour that you are open and available to your customers.

Here's a term I have shared with clients and share with you for your consideration: "Empathy fatigue." During these moments of crisis, customers call in with complaints or questions because they are afraid that they are not going to be able to get the product, medication, or service that you have been offering for years. Or they have concerns about being introduced to a new product, new medication, new service. These are some of the most challenging conversations your CSPs will have. What do these customers need in the moment? The #1 thing they will need is a lot of listening.

Your CSPs are going to do a lot of listening. They will hear sad stories, disappointment, and frustration. Be aware that they might develop empathy fatigue. It's important that you and other leaders in your organization create innovative ways to address empathy fatigue. Start by making everyone aware of this concept.

If you take my recommendation and hire an external consultant to help you implement Extreme Customer Service training, be open to hearing a different perspective on your customer service delivery. For example, you might learn that your team is not where it needs to be in terms of empathy or where you want them to be in terms of their listening skills. If you make this or another similar discovery, the next step is to prioritize training that addresses these topics.

When the critical situation is over, you will have a new list of training requirements and training topics. Extreme Customer Service, the service that you provide during a critical event, is an opportunity for you to discover how you can take your team and your organization to the next level. Do this the right way and even when there isn't a critical event, the team will know how to deliver next-level customer service every day.

CHAPTER 8

LET'S TALK ABOUT QUALITY QUALITY

A CONVERSATION WITH JEFFREY NEWMAN
Manager, Customer Care
Porsche Cars North America, Inc.

Many thanks to the team at Gladly.com for featuring Joseph Ansanelli, Gladly CEO, interviewing Jeffrey Newman, Manager, Customer Care of Porsche Cars North America in Episode #2 of their *Radically Personal Customer Service Podcast*. When I listened to Jeffrey talk about his book concept and his passion for quality, I wanted to learn more. I was delighted to be granted the opportunity to have a conversation with Jeffrey for inclusion in *The Customer Communication Formula*.

TWO BOOKS

I really must start out with our connection. Here I am writing *The Customer Communication Formula* and Jeffrey is writing *Quality Quality* about assessing and promoting the quality of customer service. It's as though we planned this. My book is scheduled for publication in 2020, and Jeffrey's current plan is to publish in 2021. I'm using notes gleaned from over 20 years to write my book. He's using notes gleaned from over 10 years to write his. And we're both huge music fans. All this made our conversation flow easily, and now I am happy to share some of Jeffrey's wisdom with you.

I was very curious about Jeffrey's book title with the double use of the word "quality," so I asked him to explain why he chose that title. His reason made total sense: it is important to ensure the quality of your Quality Assurance Program—so Quality Quality became his book title. He says companies can have excellent plans and training, but the next step is putting that plan into action to deliver quality service—in other words, making the good training stick. Jeffrey says some companies understand quality, but they aren't necessarily incorporating a *quality* quality program. Oftentimes, companies are just "checking the box."

Who is Jeffrey Newman and what does he do?

Jeffrey's background has prepared him well for his work with Porsche Cars North America. His experience came from roles with Walmart, wireless telecom Alltel, and American Express. He's a contact center expert. He's an IVR expert. He does it all. With all that, he's pretty clear about one thing: *Who* he is. Jeffrey Newman is a husband, father, and man of faith (another connection for us). *What* he does is drive for quality in his contact centers as the contact center manager. He leads people who have contact with customers.

Hiring

Jeffrey has a philosophy about the people he hires and works with. He thinks they need to enjoy their jobs. Life's too short for work you don't like. He says he has a very specific approach for talking with new hires. In the first few days on the job, he gets in front of them and explains what Porsche does, what their department does, and his expectations of them. He explains that he values *conversations* over *transactions*. He describes the relationship between the Customer Care team member and the customer as similar to doctor and patient. The team member listens, questions, and gathers facts to find a solution. He's clear that there may be "unlearning" involved if the new employee had prior contact center experience. He's also adamant that if a team member is no longer enjoying their work, they should talk to someone about this. He added that since we spend a large portion of our lives at work, we should be happy in our roles.

Team member buy-in

When I talked to him about getting team member buy-in, Jeffrey's quick response was that his general rule for everything was to have a servant's heart. He said his role was to support people in their work. He learned an important lesson about leadership from a quote used by Eddie Robinson, the late Grambling State University football coach. He said, "People don't care how much you know until they know how much you care." As a leader, Jeffrey lives by the Platinum Rule: Treat others as they want to be treated.

What he wants his team to remember is to start every conversation with a customer on the phone with a warm welcome and genuine connection. He cautions his team about jumping right to fact-gathering. He uses the analogy of speaking with your grandmother. He says if your grandmother called about a flat tire, would you begin with a question about which tire? I appreciated this analogy as I have applied a similar measure in my training and referred to my Uncle Buddy. How would I respond to my Uncle Buddy? I would start with a genuine connection.

Challenges of our virtual environments

When we talked about the challenges presented by the current global crisis and the transition to remote teams, Jeffrey made these points:

- Adoption of a virtual workforce started before the pandemic, though not all companies were fully prepared.

- Necessity advances us as people, and we are adapting for the long haul of our current reality and beyond.

- With regard to building a home-based workforce, he says it's all about adapting and adopting rules for the new environment, plus providing the extra support that teams need.

- He added that it's important to ensure consistency in leadership, whether teams are on-site, remote, or a mix of both.

- He reiterated the importance of helping and supporting team members in virtual environments. And turning off the computer after work.

Expected changes

One of the most fascinating parts of our conversation centered around changes leaders expect contact center team members to make in a year. He asked how many identifiable changes our significant other would say we made over the last year—one, two, three, more? Then he asked about the average number of coaching sessions in a quality assurance program, focusing on "what could you have done better?" At an average of five sessions a month, that means 60 things to change in a year. That is a startling comparison between the number of changes we make a year in our personal lives and what we are asking of the team. By focusing on so many changes, are we setting up our people for failure?

Advice from Jeffrey

Here's a sample of Jeffrey's advice:

- Allow people to "fail." There's more to learn in a "failure" than can be learned during side-by-side shadowing.
- Blame process and procedures, not people.
- Listen to cues from customers for how they want to be treated.
- If you are checklist-based, you aren't "in the moment," making it a challenge to have a connection with the customer.
- Build your compensation system around encouraging the human skills you want to see.
- Build your systems to fit people skills.
- Identify skills that are important *for your organization*.

A "Newmanism" using art

Jeffrey's favorite way to describe designing a Quality Assurance Program is quite artistic. Literally. Think of Van Gogh and Picasso, he says. Two distinct styles. Really unalike. Yet they were friends and in the same profession. They carried out their work quite differently from each other and both have (now) been immortalized though quite different in style. A Quality Assurance Program should be like a blank canvas for each team member—never checklist driven. Give clear guidance but allow the team members to be artists.

What's in the future?

I asked Jeffrey his thoughts as we plan for what's ahead for Customer Care. He says we can plan for:

- More use of technology as computers get smarter.

- A push toward automation, self-service, but still leaving the more complex, important things for humans to handle.
- Soft skills still needing to be the foundation of your customer-facing organization.

Quality Quality

I look forward to Jeffrey's book even more so after our conversation. I was involved in a client situation not long ago where I could have used his advice. Once clients know the 3-F Formula, know the standards, know the preferred phrases, know the benefits, the next step is delivering at that best-in-class level. That means to focus on quality, engagement, and consistency in delivery. Jeffrey will help us with that with his book *Quality Quality—Building a Quality Assurance Program That Changes Employees' Lives and Improves Your Customer Experience.*

*My sincere appreciation to Jeffrey Newman
and Porsche Cars North America, Inc.
for the opportunity to have this conversation
and share Jeffrey's insights about quality.*

PART THREE

THE 3-F FORMULA IN ACTION

CHAPTER 9

THE 3-F FORMULA SUCCESS STORIES

The conversation with Jeffrey Newman of Porsche Cars North America, Inc. in the preceding chapter is informative, insightful, and inspiring. A company with a legendary brand is automatically expected to offer exceptional customer care. Today, all companies must be mindful of the importance of customer service delivery, whether they are a legendary brand or not.

I can use my business as an example. My clients continue to comment about how I don't just teach them about customer service, I use the principles when I interact with them. I practice what I teach. As a result, my clients do most of the "selling" for me.

NEARLY 100 PERCENT OF MY CONTRACTS HAVE COME THROUGH REFERRALS, RECOMMENDATIONS, OR REPEAT BUSINESS BECAUSE I HAVE IMPLEMENTED THE 3-F'S IN MY BUSINESS.

In this chapter, you get to hear from my clients directly as they share their customer service success stories. Their stories are much like mine—they use the formula for business and in their personal lives as well.

Corporate Leader Offers "White Glove" Customer Service

When Linda Jordon, the head of a customer service organization in a multinational company, reached out to me, she already had a lot going for her and her team. She was successfully leading a team of highly qualified individuals who were excited about providing excellent customer service. Because Linda wanted her team to reach the next level, she contacted me to help identify areas of opportunity.

The opportunity

This is a quote from Linda about her experience with the 3-F Formula and during our program development:

> "Charlotte's effective coaching skills and useful techniques gave my team and me what we needed to provide our customers with 'white glove' treatment over the phone. Charlotte and I spent many days and evenings working together to ensure we had measures in place to provide the highest quality of customer service. In addition to Charlotte providing my team with one-to-one coaching, we partnered together to create other programs to assist the customer service leaders. One of my favorite programs we worked on was 'Expect to Win,' based on the book by the same name, written by Carla A. Harris."
>
> LINDA R. JORDON
> LRJ Coaching & Business Solutions, LLC
> www.lindajordon.com

It was a pleasure to work with Linda and her team because they were highly motivated, supportive of each other, and committed to doing their part to provide excellent customer service to each and every customer.

The result

Together Linda and I created strong, powerful quality assurance measures and metrics for her team to track. Linda reports that she continues to use many of the phrases and tips she learned in our training in her new career where she coaches and trains leaders.

What I really appreciate about this success story is how it shows the power of the 3-F Formula. Not only was the formula helpful at work, it contributed to the team members' personal development as well.

Custom Customer Service Training Transforms Contact Center

When the leaders of a contact center for a pharmaceutical company contacted me to inquire about collaborating to offer a custom training and development program for their team, I jumped at the opportunity to help.

The opportunity

The contact center project manager and I developed training modules and a companion handbook. We filmed videos using contact center talent to demonstrate the best practices approved by the organization. The self-guided online program is a welcome solution for training remote CSPs.

The result

When asked about the usefulness of the course, 92% of the participants responded "extremely useful" or "very useful." The CSPs requested additional one-to-one coaching for their development.

And the organization is now exploring how to roll the course out to additional contact centers throughout this multinational company.

Here are selected comments taken from the formal evaluation:

- The style of presentation is modern, well thought out, and well produced. I especially liked examples of correct terms and phrases to use such as "My apologies" and "My pleasure."
- This training program was a really good reminder of how we should be speaking with customers!
- I thought the scenarios Charlotte and [the project leader] incorporated in the modules were applicable to the content.
- It was great. I've worked in my role for many years and have been implementing most of the learning from this course. But I had forgotten some items and/or had been implementing them without really understanding the outcome of these actions to our patients.
- I thought the course was concise and very useful for someone in a customer service role. It was also very engaging.
- I think this course is a great addition to our training curriculum for all staff and hope that it has great uptake across contact centers.
- Thank you, these learning modules applied to me and my duties directly.
- This was great! The content was thorough and the examples brought the content to life. We should do more of these.

One thing that is significant to me in these comments and in many others is that CSPs welcome and appreciate interactive training that helps them do their job well and grow professionally.

The BERIQISU Story

When I had occasion to place a customer order with BERIQISU, I thought about why I was so excited to do so. From the initial visit to the website to the arrival of my order, I felt like I was part of something that went beyond the masks (facial coverings) that I ordered.

Since I was writing a book on Customer Service, I decided to contact the company so I could learn more. I am ever so glad I did.

I "interviewed" Belkis Whyte, the Designer + Founder and here's what I learned about her approach to customer service and customer connections.

1. Belkis is BERIQISU. In fact BERIQISU (pronounced berry-keé-sue or Berry 🍓 - Key 🔑 - Sue 👩) is her birth name.

2. She tells her story on her website and draws the customer to her brand. The phonetic pronunciation of her business name with the images is absolutely brilliant. Belkis says she was inspired by her upbringing in Boston, her heritage in Ghana, and her experiences as a designer in New York City.

3. Belkis enjoys having conversations with customers. She says she is completely "hands on" and her business is fully owner-driven. Since she is the business, she is laser-focused on customer satisfaction. She says she has made her "biggest discoveries" during those conversations. As a customer and a consultant, I was impressed with her listening skills and follow-through after our conversation.

4. My five masks arrived and when I opened the envelope, I found them neatly packaged in a see-through bag with all the bright colors in full view. The masks are branded with the company name on one side of the tag and a reminder that they were *handmade in New York* on the other. Nice touch.

5. As I mentioned to Belkis, there's something else she's doing that helps her customers connect with her company. I'll leave it to the branding experts to determine her secret sauce. I'll just

ask questions: Is it that she has taken mask design (facial coverings) to a whole new level? Maybe it's the colors that appear throughout her website? The photo of herself wearing her own designs? That top celebrities are customers? The simplicity of her website? That she maintains a commitment to Ghana and provides financial and in-kind contributions to the local schools in Accra? That you just want to cheer her on so she can continue to be successful? Or is it all of the above and more?

As a Customer Service Enthusiast, I am enthusiastic about the BERIQISU approach and know there's a lot that we can all learn about customer service and customer connections from this owner-driven business. (https://beriqisu.com/pages/roots).

ARE YOU AN EMPLOYEE?

What can you learn from Belkis about delivering excellent customer service?

How would your customer service approach differ if you were the owner of the company?

ARE YOU AN ENTREPRENEUR?

What can you learn from Belkis about delivering excellent customer service?

How can you use the Belkis approach to strengthen your customer connections?

CHAPTER 10

THE FORMULA AND ME

What you get by achieving your goals is not as important
as what you become by achieving your goals.
HENRY DAVID THOREAU

MY TUSCALOOSA STORY

I am writing this book so my current clients and "virtual" clients can learn more about the 3-F Customer Communication Formula. In the process, I am learning too. In fact, I'm surprised at how much I've learned about myself through this process. Writing this book has helped me become even more enthusiastic about customer service and even more grateful for the opportunities I have to share my 3-F Formula.

My clients know that I am super-serious about how we treat customers. They also know that I am passionate about creating opportunities for CSPs to grow and develop their skills. And it is likely they have learned about my love of music—I typically mention music, play music, or even have them sing to warm up their voices (but not when they are on a call with a customer).

Oh, and they will likely be able to answer the question, "Where is she from?" This is because I am highly creative in finding ways to mention my beloved Tuscaloosa, Alabama.

I hope what I share will motivate you to discover what really drives your passion for Customer Service. Everything links to the themes that have been the background music of my life:

- Manners
- Courtesy
- Humility
- Respect
- Taking turns
- Sharing and caring
- Going the extra mile
- Walking in their shoes
- Helping somebody along the way
- Using God-given talents
- Representing our own communities well
- Making the world a better place

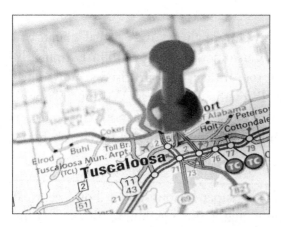

These were among the many lessons I learned in my hometown of Tuscaloosa, Alabama. I heard these words from our parents, I heard them at church, I heard them at school, and I also heard them throughout my community. As I reflect on my childhood, I realize now that this was one of the greatest blessings I could have been given. It was as though the adults got together and decided what lessons they were going to teach the next generation. These themes have served me well throughout my life and career.

I later became interested in learning more about human relationships and how people communicate with each other. My interest in this subject grew during my college years. A dear friend from college was kind enough to share this:

> When Charlotte and I were students at the University of Wisconsin-Madison, I strongly encouraged her to become a published author. I knew she had a message to share about how people interact and communicate with each other. *The Customer Communication Formula* is well worth the wait. This book is full of lessons, insights, stories, questions, and bonuses—all of which will help take your customer service to the next level. I'm so pleased that my dear friend Charlotte wrote this book, about this topic, for this time.
>
> CAROLYN ABRAMS
> Georgia

Ultimately my interests lead me to a career in Customer Service. What I have noticed on this journey, and in developing my career skills for that matter, is that when I used the principles I learned growing up in Tuscaloosa, I was able to communicate with people from diverse backgrounds, teach others how to communicate effectively, and develop a formula for customer communication.

The principles I learned in Tuscaloosa really do matter. How we treat people, whether in a personal relationship or a business relationship, is key to success in life. And it was clear that we were to treat people with respect, whatever their standing in life. I put the life lessons and professional experiences together into the 3-F Formula. This is the formula for my life and my business. It is a formula for my clients as well as other organizations and corporations.

An expectation—Show respect for service providers

A university leader once shared that the people who provided facility services felt ignored. It was as though they were invisible to others. I already had a personal "policy" about being respectful to service providers (another lesson our parents taught us). Even so, I became more intentional about showing respect and expressing appreciation to service providers after hearing the leader's comment.

I also stepped it up with hotel housekeepers. We have had some memorable conversations. We share personal stories, have moments of true connection (especially when I'm at a class reunion in Tuscaloosa and am speaking with a hotel housekeeper). I enjoy completing surveys and recognizing them for their service. While I've been blessed to have some great experiences as a Customer Service Consultant, I count it among my highest honors to receive a "thank you" note from a hotel housekeeper.

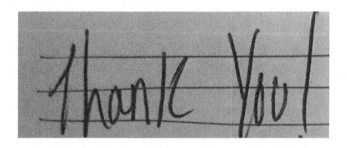

My "travels"

One of my favorite travel shows, Joseph Rosendo's *Travelscope* on PBS, ends each episode with this wisdom: *"Travel is fatal to prejudice, bigotry, and narrow-mindedness."*

As a tribute to My Awesome Clients, I'll share that being a Customer Service Consultant has allowed me to "travel" throughout corporations, small businesses, churches, campuses, and community organizations. And in some cases, I've traveled into my clients' homes and offices. In my travels, I have been *required* to learn, grow, and adapt in ways that I could not have imagined. My life (not just my business) has been greatly enriched as a result.

The Tuscaloosa lessons are being passed on

So, I take the lessons that I learned first in Tuscaloosa and I teach them to my clients (and we use them in my family too). My clients use the lessons with their customers (and their children, family members, colleagues, and friends). Millions of interactions later and the 3-F Formula is still being used—and it still works.

Charlotte has been a valuable communication resource over the past 7 years. She has such a comfortable yet accountable style that has resulted in tremendous growth with my own communication skill set as well as with the customer service acumen of the call centers I am responsible for. Her programs have greatly improved how new managers are trained for my patient access programs, how our leaders identify and grow talent, and how the customer service teams serve our customers in an effective and professional manner.

NOAH HOLMES
Head of Patient Access Services
Pharma-Biotech Industry
North Carolina

 FROM MY NOTEBOOK

CHILDREN OF CLIENTS

One of the highest compliments I've received from clients is when they ask me to offer coaching programs for their children. What a privilege to help high schoolers, college students, and young adults develop their communication skills, customer service capabilities, and confidence. This has indeed been a pleasant surprise outcome of my client relationships.

What's next for me

It is an honor to share *The Customer Communication Formula* with My Awesome Clients and all of my new "clients" who are reading this book. As a next step, I will:

- Help organizations boost their customer service brand by using the 3-F Formula
- Provide leadership for Extreme Customer Service
- Engage in 1:1 customer service conversations and calibration sessions with organizational leaders
- Share insights from *The Customer Communication Formula* and my experience as a consultant during:
  - Podcasts
  - Webinars
  - Keynotes
- Seek opportunities to serve in advisory roles on foundation and corporate boards with a special interest in programs and services for:
  - People living in public housing communities
  - People living with HIV (PLWHIV)
  - Patients needing assistance with the cost of medications
  - People in my beloved Tuscaloosa, Alabama, and in other communities in Alabama

For additional information about what's next for me and how organizations are using the 3-F Formula, please visit CharlottePurvis.com.

AFTERWORD

In the late 1990s, I had the privilege of being on the support team for a family member living with HIV/AIDS. This was a deeply personal (and emotional) experience that I took seriously. I had a mission statement, a vision statement, and a set of expectations and goals for him. It was as though I was helping to manage a program for a *group of people* living with HIV/AIDS.

Upon reflection, I realize that the experience with our family member served as training for my role as a Customer Service Consultant. I think of the different customer interactions I have influenced over the two decades for people from so many different backgrounds, adults representing all of the generations, people with just about every level of education and literacy, those who reminded me of people I know from my beloved Alabama, and people who sounded like they were truly the salt of the earth. They were patients, consumers, business partners, healthcare professionals, parents, people with critical health challenges, people who just wanted someone to listen to them, and those facing other life issues that would likely leave you speechless.

I want for all of them what I wanted for our family member—for them to be heard, to be shown empathy, to be treated with respect, and to know that we are committed to advocating for them.

When we think of Customer Service, we often think of procedures, processes, protocol. Customer Service is so much more. As Customer Service Professionals, organizational leaders, and consultants, we have an opportunity to influence organizations, to change lives, to be a blessing, and to make the world a better place. Just as I learned in my beloved Tuscaloosa, Alabama.

I'm all in.

Charlotte Purvis

THE LAST WORD

Seeing Mom's words on paper means a great deal to us.

Mom was born in Alabama and grew up during a critical time in history. Throughout our lives, she shared a lot of catchy sayings, terms, and phrases from that era. Her topics ranged from health (that's your first wealth) to taking responsibility for your actions and your inaction. Mom and Dad taught us lessons about treating people with respect, caring for people in need, and customer service. To see Mom's words about customer service on paper means a great deal to us. Now she can touch more people and share some of the lessons she taught us.

From us and Dad and our families: This is a great read, and we hope you have enjoyed it!

FAVORITE SON JAMAL
FAVORITE DAUGHTER JAMILAH
North Carolina

ABOUT THE AUTHOR

CHARLOTTE PURVIS
CharlottePurvis.com

Charlotte Purvis is a Customer Service Consultant, trainer, coach, speaker, and enthusiast. She developed the Customer Communication Formula and has tested it for over 20 years with clients in corporate, campus, and community settings. Her programs have influenced literally millions of customer interactions.

Charlotte practices what she teaches. She has a special way of developing relationships with her clients and is super-courteous when she is the customer. Her customer service programs are known for being interactive, insightful, and inspiring. She thoroughly enjoys connecting with Customer Service Professionals, learning from them, and providing feedback for their development.

Charlotte holds B.S. and M.S. degrees from the University of Wisconsin-Madison. She has served in training, leadership, and teaching roles at Iowa State University, North Carolina A&T State University, North Carolina Department of Human Resources, and North Carolina Central University.

Charlotte lives in the Research Triangle Park area of North Carolina. She enjoys going home to her beloved Tuscaloosa, Alabama, to see family and friends, to go back to the church she attended as a child, and to attend her class reunions.

NOTES

NOTES

NOTES

NOTES

NOTES

NOTES

Made in United States
North Haven, CT
16 April 2024

51393026R00095